AMSTERDAM

Research Manager
Linda Buehler

Managing Editor
Chris Kingston

Editor
Spencer Burke

Contents

Discover Amsterdam 3

Planning Your Trip 9

Accommodations 29

Sights 49

Food 73

Nightlife 94

Arts and Culture 115

Shopping 125

Essentials 132

Amsterdam 101 151

Beyond Tourism 159

Index 171

Discover Amsterdam

Tell someone you're going to Amsterdam, and you'll be met with a chuckle and a knowing smile. Yes, everyone will think you're going for the hookers and weed, but there's much more to Amsterdam. The Netherlands's permissive attitudes are the product of a long history of liberalism and tolerance that dates back far before the advent of drug tourism and prostitutes' unions. A refuge for Protestants and Jews in the 16th and 17th centuries, Amsterdam earned tremendous wealth as the center of a trading empire that stretched from the New York (sorry: New Amsterdam) to Indonesia. The city's wealth served as an incubator for the artistic achievements of the Dutch Golden Age and the economic and political birth of modern Europe. Today, Amsterdam is a diverse and progressive city as famous for its art museums and quaint canal-side cafes as for its coffeeshops and prostitution.

As you stroll the streets, savor the culture and vitality of this pretty city. You can walk or bike it in a day, moving from the peaceful canals of the Jordaan to the gaudy peepshows of the Red Light District. Old trading money lives on in graceful mansions, while, a few blocks away, repurposed squats house clubs and cinemas. Whether you're obsessed with van Gogh, want to dance all night at GLBT clubs, or always wanted to learn all about the history of fluorescent art, you're guaranteed to have a good time in Amsterdam.

Budget Amsterdam

BEYOND THE COFFEESHOP

Eat well without paying well at these five *Let's Go* picks.

- ▶ **VAN DOBBEN:** This old-school deli offers the best value in pricey Rembrandtplein, hands down (p. 84).

- ▶ **ZUIVERE KOFFIE:** A cozy cafe in the Central Canal Ring that serves up homemade croissants, sandwiches, and the best apple pie in the country (p. 81).

- ▶ **ALBERT HEIJN:** This conveniently ubiquitous supermarket chain is the best place to stock up on cheap noms.

- ▶ **CAFE DE PIJP:** Come to this De Pijp hotspot for drinks, people-watching, and affordable Middle Eastern- and Italian-inspired cuisine (p. 90).

- ▶ **'T KUYLTJE:** A no-frills take-out counter (p. 79) with delicious, filling Belgian *broodjes* (sandwiches). Yep, if you're poor in Amsterdam, you eat a lot of sandwiches.

BUNKING ON A BUDGET

It can seem like Amsterdam has a hostel for every stoned college kid in town. Here's your guide to the five best places to go Dutch.

- ▶ **FLYING PIG UPTOWN:** Stay at this popular backpacker haunt to get the Amsterdam party-hostel experience, right next to the center of the action in Leidseplein (p. 46).

- ▶ **SHELTER CITY:** Cozy and friendly, this Christian hostel is a great place to sleep in peace and avoid the weed-drenched party-hardy college kids who fill many of Amsterdam's hostels (p. 30).

- ▶ **AIVENGO YOUTH HOSTEL:** So close to Centraal Station you can taste it, this is a convenient place to stay if you're getting in late or leaving early (p. 34).

- ▶ **STAYOKAY AMSTERDAM VONDELPARK:** With 200 hostelmates, you could form your own commune here (p. 45).

Freebies

If you know where to go, it's possible to see some of the best of Amsterdam without paying a euro-penny.

- ▶ **VONDELPARK:** Wander 120 acres of rolling streams, leafy trees, and inviting grass (p. 67).

- ▶ **HOFJES:** Explore the free-admission courtyard gardens of the Jordaan (p. 64).

- ▶ **CONCERTS:** Two of the city's premier concert venues, the Concertgebouw and the Muziektheater, offer free 30min. concerts on weekdays during the summer (p. 116).

- ▶ **VONDELPARK AGAIN:** Make sure to come back here for the free summertime music and theater shows (p. 67).

- ▶ **ALBERT CUYPMARKT:** Take in local flavor at this huge market. Free to look, almost free to buy (p. 128).

- **BOB'S YOUTH HOSTEL:** Bob's is an alternative hostel hangout with graffitied walls and guitar-strumming travelers (p. 34).

SIGHTSEEING ON THE CHEAP

Amsterdam is one of the museum capitals of the world. While you're distracted by illogical spellings and trying to figure out exactly what a tram is, you might not notice how much you're spending to see everything. Relax, we've got your back.

- **MUSEUMJAARKAART:** First of all, just admire how many vowels they fit into one word there. Then rush to buy one of these if you're planning on going to more than two or three museums while you're in the city (p. 49).

- **RENT A BIKE:** Renting a bike (about €10 per day) is one of the cheapest, best, and most Dutch ways to see the city (p. 140).

- **OV-CHIPKAART:** Buy this card for an extra €7 and save a lot on public transportation—it's definitely worth it if you're in town for more than a couple of days (p. 140).

- **BRING A STUDENT ID:** Pretty much every museum offers a student discount.

- **IAMSTERDAM CARD:** Buy an Iamsterdam City Card and get free unlimited admission to museums and public transit as well as various other benefits. It's pricey, but could be worth it if you're going to be running from sight to sight (p. 135).

What To Do

WEIRD AND WACKY AMSTERDAM

Amsterdam earns its reputation for eccentricity with a host of out-there museums. **Electric Ladyland** (p. 63), the world's "First Museum of Fluorescent Art," will take you on an unforgettably weird trip into the bowels of "participatory art" and glowing rocks. The **Amsterdam Sex Museum** (p. 54) appropriately set in

the heart of the Red Light District, is a voyeur's (wet) dream, dedicated to the history and kitsch of sex. For a more wholesome, but equally bizarre, experience, drop by **Cat's Cabinet** (p. 62), an eccentric chronicle of all things feline. You can also hit up the art space at the **Stedelijk Museum Bureau** (p. 63)—there's no telling what you'll find in its rotating exhibit space, but it's well worth dropping by to find out.

PURPLE, ERR *BRUIN* HAZE

With the government set to ban foreigners from its famous coffeeshops, Amsterdam's reputation for vice will now rest squarely on its bars and clubs. Luckily, this city has no shortage of great venues to enjoy a drink. Tucked amid Leidseplein's sea of drunken tourists, **Weber** (p. 105) is a legitimately hip local favorite that you'd be remiss to miss. Then head to **Prik** (p. 99), the best of Amsterdam's many gay bars and one of its best bars, period. **Cafe de Engelbewaarder** (a "Guardian Angel" for beer-lovers) takes its Belgian beer selection pretty seriously—and so should you (p. 95). Then seek out the tiny, tilting 17th-century building that houses **de Sluyswacht** (p. 114) for some great day-drinking and people-watching.

THE HANGOVER III: AMSTERDAM

Amsterdam positively overflows with great spots for dancing the night away. **Studio 80** (p. 107) is the place to be on Saturday nights—full of the coolest Dutch kids, techno fanatics, and a few in-the-know tourists—while **Sugar Factory** (p. 105) is just a sweet place to dance. You can have a very good Friday (and live music any day) in the converted church that's home to **Paradiso** (p. 105). And for the best of Amsterdam crammed into one place, head to **OT301** (p. 111), a former squat that now hosts the best dubstep in the city.

BEYOND TOURISM

Ready to take a break from drinking Amstel and counting coffeeshops? Get more involved in Dutch culture by studying, working, or volunteering. Save the planet from environmental disaster and capitalist exploitation with **Friends of the Earth International** (p. 164), go Dutch with the help of one of Amsterdam's many language institutes (p. 163), or crack some ribs at **Boom Chicago** (p. 170), the city's only American comedy club.

Student Superlatives

- **MOST EMBARRASSING MUSEUM TO VISIT WITH YOUR FAMILY (ESPECIALLY CREEPY UNCLE NICK):** The Amsterdam Sex Museum (p. 54).

- **BEST PLACE TO PONDER WHY SOMEONE WOULD CUT OFF THEIR OWN EAR:** The Van Gogh Museum (p. 65).

- **BEST PLACE TO PRETEND THE '80S NEVER ENDED:** Studio 80 (p. 107).

- **BEST PLACE TO STAR IN A BEER COMMERCIAL:** The Heineken Museum (p. 68).

- **MOST OUT OF PLACE:** The statue of stately Rembrandt just can't keep up with the revelry around him in Rembrandtplein (p. 107).

Planning Your Trip

The first step to getting a handle on Amsterdam's geography is to understand its canals. The Singel wraps around the heart of the Centrum, which is made up from east to west of the Oude Zijd, Red Light District, and Nieuwe Zijd. Barely 1km in diameter, the Centrum's skinny streets overflow with bars, brothels, clubs, and tourists—many of whom won't leave this area during their whole stay in Amsterdam.

The next set of canals, running in concentric circles, are Herengracht, Keizersgracht, and Prinsengracht (hint: "gracht" means "canal", so if you're looking for a "gracht" street and you don't see water, you're lost). These enclose a somewhat classier area filled with locals, tasty restaurants, and plenty of museums (some very worthwhile, others completely ridiculous). Rembrandtplein and Leidseplein, the twin hearts of Amsterdam's and party scene, are also nestled here.

To the east of the canal ring are Jodenbuurt and Plantage, the city's old Jewish quarter. Moving southwest you get to De Pijp, an artsy neighborhood filled with immigrants and hipsters, then Museumplein and Vondelpark, home to the city's largest park and most important museums. Working back north to the west of the center you'll find Oud-West and Westerpark, two largely residential neighborhoods that are experiencing a boom in popularity and culture. In between Westerpark and the canal ring is the reliably chic Jordaan. Finally, to the north, in between Jordaan and Centraal Station, lies Scheepvaartbuurt, the city's old shipping quarter.

Icons

First things first: places and things that we absolutely love, sappily cherish, generally obsess over, and wholeheartedly endorse are denoted by the all-empowering ⚑ **Let's Go thumbs-up.** In addition, the icons scattered at the end of a listing can serve as visual cues to help you navigate each listing:

⚑	Let's Go recommends	☎	Phone numbers	✈	Directions
i	Other hard info	⑤	Prices	⏰	Hours

WHEN TO GO

Amsterdam is most thronged by tourists in July and August, and for good reason: this is when the weather is sunniest, the days are longest, and most Amsterdammers are away on vacation. The crowds are thinner and the climate stays pleasant between April and October. Come at the end of April and beginning of May to see Holland's famous tulips in bloom. Temperatures rarely rise to uncomfortable levels here, even at the height of summer, but rain and fog are common occurrences. Flights and accommodations are cheaper in the winter, when the mostly empty canals and streets frost over.

NEIGHBORHOODS

Oude Zijd

Many will delight in telling you that the Oude Zijd ("Old Side") is in fact newer than the Nieuwe Zijd ("New Side"). That doesn't really say much about the character of the neighborhood, which is sandwiched between the wild Red Light District and the more relaxed, local-dominated Jodenbuurt and feels like a balance between the two. A mini-kinda-Chinatown stretches along the northern part of **Zeedijk,** which spills into **Nieuwmarkt,** a lovely square dominated by a medieval ex-fortress. The bars and cafes lining Nieuwmarkt's perimeter are popular places for tourists and locals to rub elbows over a beer. Farther south is **Kloveniersburgwal,** a canal lined with genteel 17th-century buildings (many now occupied by the University of Amsterdam). Fancier hotels and cafes start to replace the tourist-traps and faux-British pubs where the canal hits the Amstel.

Red Light District

Once defined by the sailors who frequented Amsterdam's port, the Red Light District dates back to the 13th century, when business-savvy ladies began to capitalize on the crowds of sex-starved seamen. Today, the only sailors you'll find are the fake ones in the gay porn and costume shops, but the sex industry still flourishes here. The neighborhood is remarkably well regulated and policed, but this is definitely no Disneyland (though the number of families sightseeing here might surprise you). The **Oudezijds Achterburgwal,** with its live sex shows and porn palaces, is the Red Light's major artery. The streets perpendicular to this main thoroughfare are lined with girl-filled windows, stretching to **Oudezijds Voorburgwal** and **Warmoesstraat.** Some sex stores and theaters have set up camp on these western streets, but for the most part they provide bars for male tourists to get liquored up before venturing through one of the neon-lit doors. Those not looking for prostitution can still carouse in the Red Light District's endless sea of bars and coffeeshops. You'll also find an immense army of the infamous Dutch public urinals, as well as the type of traveler who feels comfortable using them. To see the hedonism at its peak, come on a Friday or Saturday night; for a less overwhelming visit, try strolling through on a weekday afternoon.

Nieuwe Zijd

Older than the Oude Zijd (but home to a church that's younger than the Oude Kerk, thus explaining the neighborhoods' confusing name swap), the Nieuwe Zijd offers a mix of history, culture, and a whole lot of tourists. **Damrak,** its eastern edge, stretches from **Centraal Station** to **Dam Square** and then turns into **Rokin.** These are some of the busiest streets in the city, full of souvenir shops and shawarma stands; they're best tackled on foot, as this is the one part of Amsterdam where bikes don't rule the road. As you head west to **Spuistraat,** the streets become less crowded and more hip. **Kalverstraat,** one of the city's prime shopping streets for centuries, is now home to department stores and international chains. The Nieuwe Zijd is tourist central, full of huge hostels and coffeeshops, and you're much more likely to run into drug-ready backpackers and elderly tourists taking pictures than any locals.

Scheepvaartbuurt

Scheepvaartbuurt, which would create quite a round on *Wheel of Fortune,* is Amsterdam's old shipping quarter. It was traditionally a working-class neighborhood with a lot of immigrants and had a reputation as one of the rougher parts of the city. Nowadays, despite looking difficult to pronounce (it's actually not that bad... it's like "shape-fart-burt"), Scheepvaartbuurt is a pleasant area full of young people and largely devoid of tourists. Remnants of the neighborhood's salty seadog past—like bronze propellers, anchors, and steering wheels—dot the sidewalks, and you can almost detect a faint whiff of the sea breeze that once blew ships to this shore. There aren't any real sights, but it's worth a visit for the local shops that line **Haarlemmerplein,** which becomes **Haarlemmerdijk** as you move east toward residential Westerpark.

Canal Ring West

The Canal Ring West lies around—spoiler alert—a ring of three canals: the **Herengracht, Keizersgracht,** and **Prinsengracht** (helpful hint: they go in alphabetical order from the center of the city toward the west). It extends from Brouwersgracht in the north down to the Leidseplein. Chock-full of grand canal houses and quaint houseboats, the neighborhood provides a nice escape from the more crowded Nieuwe Zijd next door. Three major sights draw visitors: the **Anne Frank House, Westerkerk,** and the **Homomonument.** The **Nine Streets,** small lanes running from the Prinsengracht to the Singel, south of Raadhuisstraat, are packed with more unique stores and vibrant cafes than we can fit in this guidebook.

Central Canal Ring

The Central Canal Ring tends to get overshadowed by its neighbors: Museumplein outshines its sights, Rembrandtplein and Leidseplein outdo its nightlife, and De Pijp offers a more exciting culinary scene. However, this neighborhood—the area from **Leidsestraat** to the **Amstel,** bordered on the north by the

Singel and on the south by **Weteringschans**—enjoys the best parts of its surrounds without suffering their crowds, high prices, and soul- and cash-sucking tourist traps. **Utrechtsestraat** in particular offers lively cafes, restaurants, and stores, all frequented by a mix of locals and tourists, while the **Golden Bend** boasts some of Amsterdam's most impressive architecture. Along the Southern border, **Weteringplantsoen** and **Frederiksplein** provide some small but pretty green spaces to stop and rest your feet.

Leidseplein

The Leidseplein, an almost exclusively commercial rectangle south of the Central Canal Ring, has a polarizing effect on those who pass through it, inspiring either devotion or disapproval. It's a busy, toristy part of town that lies in the area between the Nassaukade, Spiegelgracht, Prinsengracht, and Leidsegracht. During the day, the square is packed with street performers and promoters for pub crawls and other assorted evening entertainments. At night, the revelry continues in a bath of neon light and cheap beer. The few streets running through the Leidseplein's interior are packed with ethnic restaurants, theaters, bars, and clubs. Among the sushi and salsa, there are also a number of very Dutch establishments to be found. Numerous transport connections, including the elusive night bus, make this neighborhood a convenient as well as fun part of town. There are no sights to speak of, though look out for the enigmatic inscription *"Homo sapiens non urinat in ventum"* ("A wise man does not piss into the wind") on the pillars above **Max Euweplein Square.** While many Dutch will frown in pity if you spend much of your trip here, the best part about Leidseplein is that some of those frown-bearers will secretly be living it up here all weekend, too.

Rembrandtplein

For our purposes, the Rembrandtplein neighborhood comprises the square itself, plus the area stretching from Herengracht to the Amstel, and the part of Reguliersdwarstraat between Vijzelstraat and the Bloemenmarkt. Once upon a time (a.k.a. the late 17th century), the area now known as Rembrandtplein was home to Amsterdam's butter market *(Botermarkt)*. The construction of a few hotels in the 20th century brought tourists, and with the tourists came booze (and euro-trance). With a few noteworthy exceptions, food and accommodations in Rembrandtplein often cost more than they're worth. The real reason to come here is the nightlife. Rembrandtplein's bars and clubs are as popular and numerous as in the Leidseplein, but tend to be larger and more exclusive, with more locals and GLBT establishments. Europe's largest LCD TV screen, located above Amsterdam's largest club, **Escape,** lights up the square at night. From the middle of the square, a statue of **Rembrandt van Rijn** looks benevolently down at the madness. When you get tired of bar-hopping, take a rest in nearby **Thorbeckeplein,** a grassy stretch of trees, named for Johan Rudolph Thorbecke (1798-1872), known colloquially as the first prime minister of the Netherlands. "Thorbeckeplein" is also the name of a song written by the popular Dutch singer Robert Long about a bittersweet gay love affair.

Jordaan

Once a staunchly working-class neighborhood, the Jordaan has been transformed into one of Amsterdam's prettiest and most fashionable areas. It provides a nice escape from the overwhelming hordes of tourists in the Red Light District to its east and has more energy than the more residential Westerpark to the (what do you think?) west. Streets are narrow, canals are leafy, and gabled houses are clumped together in colorful rows. You won't find any of Amsterdam's most famous sights here (well, except for **Electric Ladyland**), but the Jordaan's restaurants and cafes are not to be missed. Establishments in the northern part of the neighborhood are more often filled with locals, while tourists tend to wander over from Westermarkt into the area near **Rozengracht.**

Westerpark and Oud-West

Westerpark is a residential neighborhood northeast of the main city center; its eponymous park is a serene stretch of green that makes for a pleasant break from the urban jungle. It has a loyal and vocal community—just don't expect to hear any English—and is becoming increasingly popular among young people and artists, bringing ever-exciting cultural projects and nightlife to its streets. South of Westerpark lies the Oud-West, still dominated by locals but with a few large streets (**Kinkerstraat** and **Overtoom** in particular) full of small ethnic cafes and cheap chain stores that keep the area busy. The northern part of Oud-West is a little grungy, but the area farther south—north of Vondelpark, close to the Leidseplein—is probably the most tourist-friendly part of the neighborhood.

Museumplein and Vondelpark

Museumplein and Vondelpark lie just south of the main canal ring, close to the city center yet somewhat removed from its hectic nature. Vondelpark is a gorgeous green space with some fine hostels not far from the excitement of Leidseplein and the ethnic eateries of the Oud-West. Museumplein, meanwhile, feels distinctly different from the rest of the city, attracting older and more affluent tourists than the backpacker-swarmed areas to the north. **P. C. Hooftstraat** is lined with designer stores like Prada and Tiffany. But just because you're young and on a budget doesn't mean you should shy away. Museumplein is a large, grassy field lined with some of the best museums in the world—no visit to Amsterdam is complete without a trip to the **Van Gogh Museum** and **Rijksmuseum.** Most of the tourist-friendly action is sandwiched between Stadhouderskade to the north and Van Baerlestraat (which contains the Museumplein tram stop) to the south. Come here to get some space, culture, and class—three things that feel far away when you're downing Heinekens with the masses in a hostel bar on Warmoesstraat.

De Pijp

De Pijp ("duh pipe") may lack history and sights, but it more than makes up for that with modern culture. A mix of immigrants, students, and artists creates a haven of excellent ethnic restaurants, fun cafes, and relatively inexpensive housing. **Albert Cuypstraat** hosts the city's largest open-air market, along with a cluster of cafes, clothing stores, and cheap eats. Intersecting Albert Cuypstraat to the west is **Ferdinand Bolstraat,** which is home to a high concentration of restaurants and leads to the avoidable **Heineken Experience.** Still a little bit rough around the edges, De Pijp has all the charm of the Jordaan in a much younger and more urban environment.

Jodenbuurt and Plantage

A high concentration of sights and museums is the real draw here, but don't overlook the few excellent restaurants and small bars. The open space in these neighborhoods is a great antidote to the over-crowded city center. Jodenbuurt, centered around **Waterlooplein,** was historically the home of Amsterdam's Jewish population. Plantage, home to wide streets and numerous parks, stretches around Jodenbuurt to the east. Most commercial establishments can be found on the streets near the **Artis Zoo** or near the **Rembrandt House**.

SUGGESTED ITINERARIES

Let's (Van) Gogh

Forget Italy—the Dutch Golden Age inspired serious strides in architecture, literature, and painting that match the achievements of the more famous Renaissance to the south. Leonardo, Donatello, Raphael, and Michelangelo? Check out Amsterdam's finest art and history museums on this walking tour, and you'll surely agree that the Ninja Turtles should have been named Rembrandt, Vermeer, Hals, and Brueghel.

1. VAN GOGH MUSEUM. Take your time as you look at sunflowers and ear wounds: this is the best museum in the city (p. 65).

2. RIJKSMUSEUM. Step next door to the Rijksmuseum, which is not nearly as imposing as it looks. Only part of the collection is on display until renovations are completed in 2013, but it's still worth a visit (p. 66).

3. GOLDEN BEND. Walk through the Central Canal Ring, checking out the stately old 17th-century mansions of the **Golden Bend**. Stop by the **Museum Willet-Holthuysen** (p. 62) to see inside one of these old houses, then check out the **FOAM** (photography museum; p. 61).

4. NIEUWE ZIJD. Continue on through the center of town to the **Amsterdam Historical Museum** (p. 55), where art and artifacts are used to illustrate the city's history. Then peek inside **Nieuwe Kerk** (p. 54) for its temporary art exhibits set against the stunning backdrop of the church's Gothic architecture.

5. REMBRANDT. Head over to Jodenbuurt to conclude your tour with the **Museum Het Rembrandt,** where you'll see Rembrandt's house and hundreds of his etchings (p. 71).

Cheap Date

Here's how to have an inexpensive, but romantic night, out in Amsterdam.

> **1. VONDELPARK MOVIE.** Take your date to see a movie at the **Vondelpark EYE** (p. 120); they sometimes screen free outdoor movies inside the city's largest park. As of 2008, it's technically legal to have sex in the park, but *Let's Go* doesn't recommend making your move quite yet.
>
> **2. DE PIJP DINNER.** Instead, head to De Pijp for a tasty, cheap dinner at **Bazar** (p. 91) or **Cafe De Pijp** (p. 90).
>
> **3. LEIDSEPLEIN DRINKS.** Saunter over to **Weber** (p. 105) in Leidsplein for a drink or two, then stroll down Korte Leidsedwarsstraat or another side street. Once you get a little away from the square (the *plein,* as it were), you can find any number of fun student bars with €1.50 beers and soundtracks that mix Top 40 with old Dutch sentimental love songs. In short, seduction central.

A Three-Day Weekend in Amsterdam

Day 1

> **Rent A Bike** (p. 140) near Centraal Station. Ask the guy at the store what the different gears are for. Learn now or learn the hard way. Ride down Haarlemmerstraat, full of cheap eats, stores, and coffeeshops; it might be the best bike ride in the universe. Then ride south through the quaint streets of Jordaan. Take a breather at a canal-side cafe; stop in at **Rainarai** (p. 85) for some Algerian takeout, admire a few **Hofjes** (p. 64), and delve into the fluorescent mad genius of **Electric Ladyland** (p. 63). Cross Prinsengracht Canal, and sober up for a visit to the famous **Anne Frank Museum** (p. 57). If your legs can handle it, climb the 85m tower of **Westerkerk** (p. 58) for the best view in the city. Feast on some Belgian sandwiches at **'t Kuyltje** (p. 79). End the night by immersing yourself in the nightlife madness of **Leidseplein** (p. 104).

Day 2

Head straight for Amsterdam's premier art museums, the **Van Gogh** and **Rijksmuseum,** both in Museumplein (p. 65). Take notes so you can convince your friends later that you didn't just come to Amsterdam to do drugs. Check out *The Potato Eaters and De Melkmeid,* but you have a lot to do today, so it's best to take them at a run. Just kidding—running is probably frowned upon. Walk briskly. Grab some food at **Pasta Tricolore** (p. 90), then head to **Vondelpark,** the prettiest park in the city, for a picnic. Stroll through the half-mile-long outdoor market, **Albert Cuypmarkt** (p. 128), then explore some of **De Pijp's** excellent restaurants (p. 90). Don't forget to try some *stroopwafel* ice cream at **Het Ijspaleis** (p. 90), then a cocktail at **Chocolate Bar** (p. 113). See a show at **Melkweg** (p. 117) to close out the day.

Day 3

Not eating breakfast is not Dutch. Grab a traditional Dutch breakfast. (Note: this is the only occasion in Dutch dining when "traditional" also means "delicious.") Try *oilbollen* (fried dough balls with raisins) or toast with chocolate sprinkle things, called *hagelslag.* Seek out bakery window-fronts with the most drool-worthy pastries. Not enough euro? Not a problem. You can find an **Albert Heijn** (p. 73) every few blocks with the same *stroopwafels* at lower prices. After breakfast, wander the classic old Amsterdam sights of the **Golden Bend** (p. 62). Head north to Nieuwe Zijd, one of the oldest parts of the city, and check out the 15th-century **Nieuwe Kerk** (p. 54). Now, choose your own museum adventure and continue to either the **Amsterdam Historical Museum** (p. 55) or the **Amsterdam Sex Museum** (p. 54). Head back to your place to rest up for a farewell tour of Amsterdam nightlife. Take in the sights on a walk through the **Red Light District** (p. 51). Have some drinks at **Weber** (p. 105) or **Festina Lente** (p. 110), then make a bee-line for **Paradiso** (p. 105) and **Studio 80** (p. 107) for the crazy best that Amsterdam has to offer.

Purchase any Eurail Pass and receive a **FREE** Hostelrescard
$18 value!

Experience the incredible diversity of European trains and long lasting impressions with Eurail Pass. Visit www.myeurailtravel.com and share your stories with the rest of the world.

With a hostelrescard you can book low cost accommodations at over 25,000 hostels, budget hotels, and Bed & Breakfasts throughout Europe. All the customary reservation, booking, and handling fees will be waived for you.

To get your FREE Hostelrescard:

Purchase your Eurail Pass from any Eurail office or travel agency. Visit **www.hostelrescard.com/eurail** and enter your Eurail ticket number. You will receive your **free** Hostelrescard by e-mail, and can begin browsing and booking inexpensive accommodations for your European trip right away.

Hostelrescard, Inc.
11043 N. Saint Andrews Way • Scottsdale, AZ 85254
info@hostelrescard.com • (480) 361-1551

www.hostelrescard.com/eurail

Attention Students: For discounts on admission to museums, attractions and sights throughout Europe, get your International Student Exchange Identity Card – ISE Card at
www.isecard.com

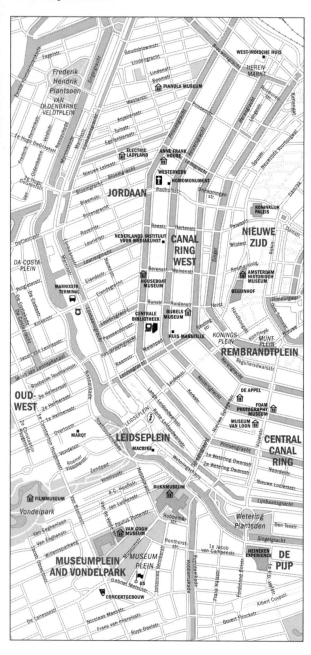

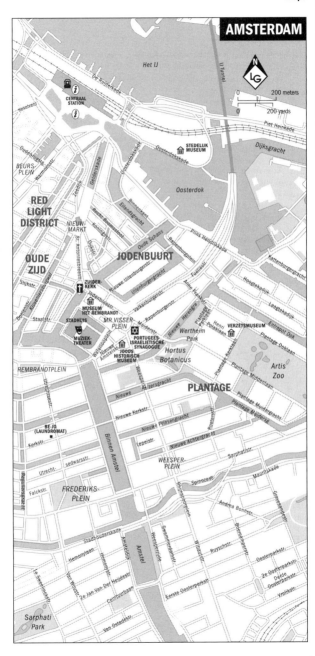

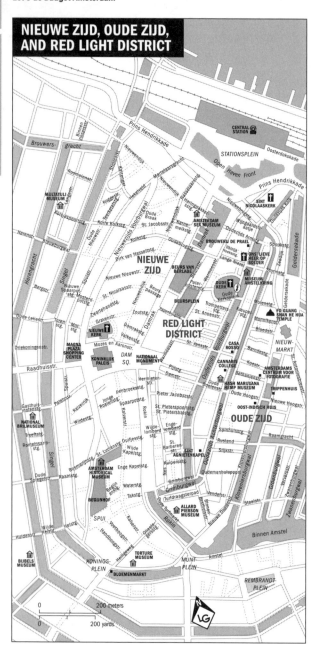

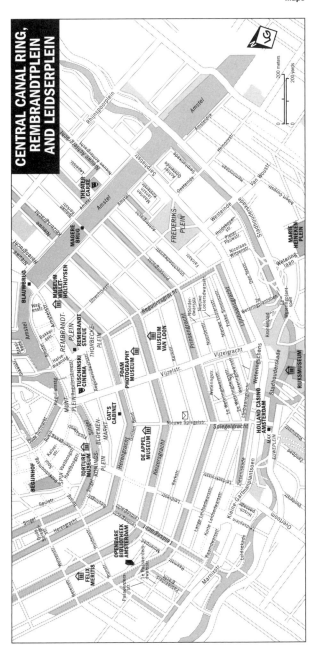

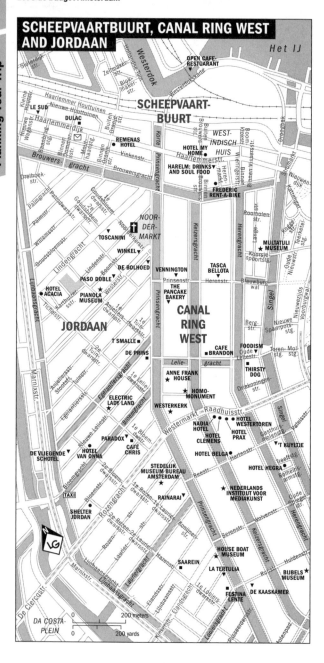

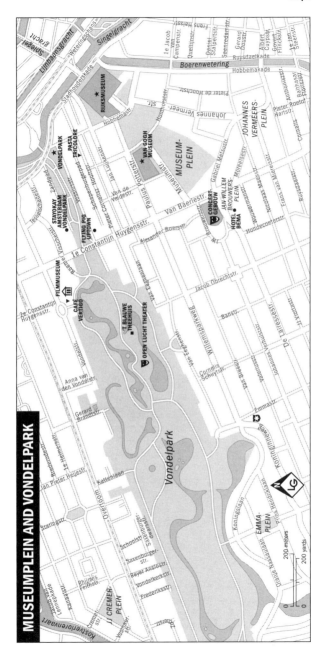

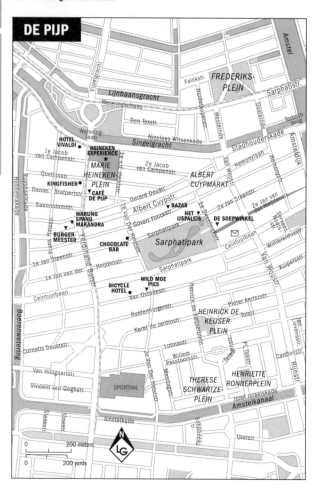

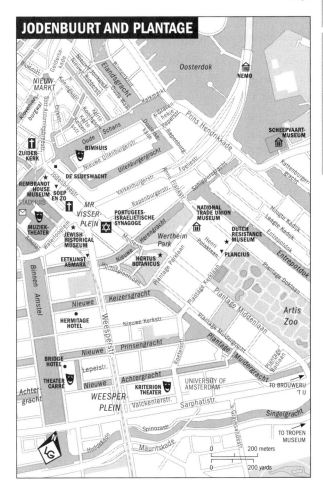

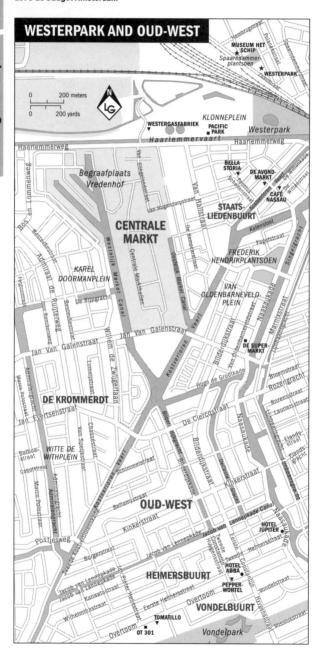

Accommodations

When lodging in Amsterdam, chances are you'll either be staying in a big backpacker hostel or a small hotel in a converted canal house. For the most part, anything you find in the city center is a decent option, but there's a huge range of value—some rooms are simply small white boxes with a bed, while others are lovingly decorated with attention to cozy details or an interesting theme. To get the most for your euro, consider staying in one of the neighborhoods outside of the main canal ring. If you didn't come to Amsterdam to find a 24hr. party, avoid hostels in the Red Light District. If you came to get down all day and all of the night, centrally located hostels, often with late-night bars attached, will provide plenty of opportunities to meet fellow travelers with similar missions.

Room rates fluctuate according to season and day of the week. The closer you get to the cold of winter, the cheaper your room will be—except for the days surrounding Christmas and New Year's, when prices skyrocket. While we don't advise showing up without having booked a room, especially during the summer, owners with too many unoccupied beds have been known to radically slash prices at less busy times.

> ## Budget Accommodations
>
> Finding budget accommodations in Amsterdam is easy: this city is full of hostels. However, finding one that suits you can be a challenge. Many may find themselves torn between rowdy, nightlife-esque hostels in Nieuwe Zijd or the Red Light District and pseudo-convent Christian hostels in outer neighborhoods like the Jordaan. This is a false dilemma. For those who want a quality, quiet room, but still want to experience Amsterdam's wild side, the hostels of Museumplein and Vondelpark are the best balance.

OUDE ZIJD

The Oude Zijd isn't home to as many accommodations as the nearby Red Light District or Nieuwe Zijd, but it's home to two of the city's best.

Shelter City   HOSTEL $
Barndesteeg 21
☎020 625 32 30; www.shelter.nl

Shelter City is a large Christian hostel (with no religious requirements for guests) in the heart of the Oude Zijd. All rooms are single-sex, most with shared baths, a few with ensuites. The beds are a bit reminiscent of those in army barracks, but the well-decorated common spaces, including a cafe, breakfast room, and courtyard garden, encourage guests to make new friends. Shelter City is popular with a wide array of young backpackers, from the quiet museum lover to the rabid party-goer.

▶ ⁂ ⓜNieuwmarkt. Just off the southwestern edge of the square. *i* Breakfast included. Free Wi-Fi. No drugs or alcohol allowed. ⓢ Beds €15-34. Discounts available for longer stays. ⓩ Security 24hr.

Stayokay Amsterdam Stadsdoelen (HI)   HOSTEL $
Kloveniersburgwal 97
☎020 624 68 32; www.stayokay.com/stadsdoelen

Enjoy professional, upbeat staff and some cushy amenities rarely found in hostels: washing and drying machines, a TV room complete with foosball table, and a substantial breakfast including fruit and cornflakes (different varieties of cornflakes!). Rooms are plain and clean in this huge hostel—with over 150 beds, look here when your whole Varsity Marching Band needs a place to stay in Amsterdam. Located in an old canal building in a tranquil part of the Oude Zijd, this hostel is nearer to Jodenbuurt but still just a short walk from Dam Sq., the Red Light District, and Rembrandtplein.

▶ Tram #4, 9, 16, 24, or 25 to Muntplein. Walk down Nieuwe Doelenstraat; Kloveniersburgwal is on the right over the bridge. *i* Breakfast included. Free Wi-Fi. Ⓢ Co-ed or single-sex 8- to 20-bed dorms €15-30, depending on season and day; private rooms €39-70. HI discount.

RED LIGHT DISTRICT

Sure, this neighborhood is obsessed with sex, but the high concentration of hotels and hostels on Warmoesstraat means that there is an industry for the less red-blooded traveler as well. These are great places to stash your pack and go unabashedly wild with fellow backpackers. While the prices vary seasonally, rates in the Red Light District also tend to fall drastically in the middle of the week.

The Greenhouse Effect Hotel   HOTEL $$$
Warmoesstraat 55
☎020 624 49 74; www.greenhouse-effect.nl

The Greenhouse Effect has some of the nicest rooms in Amsterdam, definitely miles above average for the Red Light District. Each room is decorated according to its own whimsical theme: there's "1001 Nights," with gauzy wall hangings and an exotic chandelier; the "Sailor's Cabin," done up ship-shape with deep blue walls and brass accents; and the "Outer Space" room, with a translucent neon green light-up sink, to name a few. Guests recieve discounts at the bar below and the coffeeshop next door.

▶ From Centraal Station, walk south on Damrak, turn right onto Brugsteeg, and left onto Warmoesstraat. *i* Breakfast included. Most rooms have en-suite bath. Free Wi-Fi in the bar. Ⓢ Singles €65-75; doubles €95-110; triples €130.

Durty Nelly's Hostel   HOSTEL $
Warmoesstraat 115-117
☎020 638 01 25; www.durtynellys.nl

A popular hostel over a convivial pub, Durty Nelly's boasts co-ed dorms that are (ironically) very clean. The rooms aren't terribly spacious, but they feel more cozy than cramped. Guests receive a discount at the pub below.

▶ From Centraal Station, walk south on Damrak, turn right onto Brugsteeg, and right onto Warmoesstraat. *i* Breakfast included. Free Wi-Fi. Large lockers available. ⑤ 4- to 10-bed dorms €25-50.

Hotel Winston

HOSTEL $$

Warmoesstraat 129

☎020 623 13 80; www.winston.nl

Hotel Winston feels more modern and continental than the other boozing-and-snoozing complexes on the street, thanks in part to the attached sleek bar and trendy club. Always busy, Winston fills up fast with backpackers and young people. It's not the cheapest place on the block and doesn't have the most interesting rooms, but it is perfect for larger groups and those who prefer the club scene to the pubs connected to most of Winston's competitors.

▶ ⁂ From Centraal Station, walk south on Damrak, turn right onto Brugsteeg, and right onto Warmoesstraat. *i* Breakfast included. Free Wi-Fi. ⑤ Dorms €32-40; singles €73-95; doubles €88-114.

Meeting Point Youth Hostel

HOSTEL $

Warmoesstraat 14

☎020 627 74 99; www.hostel-meetingpoint.nl

Meeting Point's location near Centraal Station and its low prices make it popular with young backpackers. Be warned: anarchy frequently reigns in the 24hr. bar downstairs. Female travelers take note that there are no single-sex dorms, and the hostel tends to attract a rowdier crowd that isn't suited for the faint of heart. Those looking for peace and quiet would do best to look elsewhere.

▶ ⁂ From Centraal Station, turn left onto Prins Hendrikkade, right onto Nieuwebrugsteeg, and right onto Warmoesstraat. *i* Breakfast €2.50. Lockers available, lock rentals €2 per stay. Free Wi-Fi. ⑤ 18-bed dorms €18-25; 8-bed €25-30.

Hotel Internationaal

HOTEL $$$

Warmoesstraat 1-3

☎020 624 55 20; www.hotelinternationaal.com

Although it's similar to other small bar-hotel setups along the street, Hotel Internationaal stands out thanks to its extra-amicable staff and pastel-green walls. The rooms are otherwise nondescript—though those on the top floor have cool Tudor-style beams—but are perfectly functional and comfortable. All rooms include a sink, while some have ensuite baths. Despite being a hotel rather than a hostel, the atmosphere is only a couple of decibels quieter than the party-hard complexes down the street.

▶ ✈ From Centraal Station, turn left onto Prins Hendrikkade, right onto Nieuwebrugsteeg, and right onto Warmoesstraat. *i* Free Wi-Fi. Computers available. Ⓢ Doubles €65-85, with bath €85-110; quads €120-140.

Hotel Vijaya
HOTEL $$

Oudezijds Voorburgwal 44
☎020 626 94 06; www.hotelvijaya.com

This hotel at the edge of the Red Light District, not far from the Oude Kerk, offers some of the cheapest private rooms in the area. Singles are somewhat small but still a bargain, especially midweek when prices fall. Breakfast is served in a spacious dining room.

▶ ✈ From Centraal Station, turn left onto Prins Hendrikkade and then bear right onto Nieuwebrugsteeg. Continue straight and Nieuwebrugsteeg will become Oudezijds Voorburgwal. *i* Breakfast included. All rooms have en-suite bath. Free Wi-Fi. Ⓢ Singles €35-80; doubles €50-105.

Old Nickel Hotel
HOTEL $$$

Nieuwebrugsteeg 11
☎020 624 19 12; www.oldquarter.com/oldnickel

At the northern tip of the Red Light District, Old Nickel remains close to the activity but maintains some peace and quiet for guests. The plaid coverlets on the beds and nature wallpaper can almost fool you into thinking you're in a British country inn—the pub downstairs certainly adds to that impression. Slanted ceilings add a nice sense of coziness to the rooms on the top floor.

▶ ✈ From Centraal Station, turn left onto the far side of Prins Hendrikkade, then turn right onto Nieuwebrugsteeg. *i* Breakfast included. All rooms have shared bath. Free Wi-Fi. Ⓢ Singles €50-75; doubles €60-85.

NIEUWE ZIJD

The Nieuwe Zijd is packed with accommodations, making it easy to stumble straight from Centraal Station into your room. Hotels here tend to be pricey, but top-notch hostels abound.

🏛 Flying Pig Downtown
HOSTEL $

Nieuwendijk 100
☎020 420 68 22; www.flyingpig.nl

A lively bar, a comfy smoking lounge, and spacious dorms make this party hostel a perennial favorite among backpackers. The youthful staff and frequent events—like live DJs, drink specials, and televised sports games—help to drive a social atmosphere. Guests are referred to as "piggies," but don't worry, it's meant to be endearing. Queen-sized bunk beds (perfect for couples, "special" friends, or maybe even "just friends") are available in some dorms and must be booked for two people.

▶ ⌗ From Centraal Station, walk toward Damrak. Pass the Victoria Hotel and take the 1st alley on the right, which leads to Nieuwendijk. *i* Breakfast included. Towels included. Kitchen available. Free Wi-Fi. Computers available. ⓢ 4- to 18-bed dorms €20-30. Significant discounts online and in the low season.

Aivengo Youth Hostel   HOSTEL $
Spuistraat 6
☎020 421 36 70; www.aivengoyouthhostel.com

Aivengo isn't just one of the closest hostels to Centraal Station—it's also one of the nicest. Deep colors and gauzy purple curtains give some dorms a decadent, *Arabian Nights* vibe, while others have clean, crisp interiors that are more reminiscent of Ikea. A mix of bunks and normal beds fills the large and sociable dorms. Somewhat humorously (misogynistically, some might say), the all-female dorms are the only ones equipped with kitchens—other dorms include only a fridge and microwave. Two private doubles are also available, one with a roof terrace and a hot tub.

▶ ⌗ From Centraal Station, walk down Martelarsgraacht and keep straight onto Hekelveld, whichbecomes Spuistraat. *i* Free Wi-Fi. Computers available. ⓢ Summer dorms €20-35; winter from €12. Private rooms €70-110.

Bob's Youth Hostel   HOSTEL $
Nieuwezijds Voorburgwal 92
☎020 624 63 58; www.bobsyouthhostel.nl

A slightly hippie-er counterpart to the Flying Pig, Bob's Youth Hostel attracts flocks of young travelers who enjoy lounging in the graffiti-filled bar and strumming their guitars outside on the steps. The dorms are decorated with cheeky, colorful murals by visiting artists. An apartment with a kitchen and bath is available for two or three people. Though it used to operate on a first-come-first-served, ultra-free-spirit-style system, the new management now accepts advance reservations.

▶ ⌗ From Centraal Station, go down Martelaarsgracht and bear left as it becomes Nieuwezijds Voorburgwal. *i* Breakfast included. Wi-Fi €3 per hr., €4 per day. Computers available. ⓢ 4- to 16-bed dorms €25-35; apartment €90-120. ☾ Bar open until 3am.

Hostel Aroza   HOSTEL $
Nieuwendijk 23
☎020 620 91 23; www.aroza.nl

Trippy murals in the halls give this place definite charm, although the "Don't Worry, Be Sexy" signs might be a little too charming for some tastes. The downstairs bar is a popular hangout and features a guestbook and colored pencils for guests to record their visit for future generations, or just so they can amuse themselves after an evening of coffeeshop-hopping.

▶ ⚓ From Centraal Station, turn right, left at Martelaarsgracht, and right onto Nieuwendijk. *i* Breakfast included. Lockers included. Single-sex and co-ed dorms available. Free Wi-Fi. Computer with internet in the bar. ⑤ Dorms €25-30.

Hotel Brouwer   HOTEL $$$
Singel 83
☎020 624 63 58; www.hotelbrouwer.nl

If you want to know what it's like to live in an old Dutch canal house, Hotel Brouwer is your best bet (and value). Each room is named for a Dutch artist, but the "Bosch" room, a small double, is the real delight, with antique furniture in the living room and a traditional box bed set into the wall. The other rooms, which all overlook the pretty Singel Canal, are less distinctive but still spacious and well decorated. All of them make for a nice change of pace from the seedier hostels and hotels of the Nieuwe Zijd.

▶ ⚓ From Centraal Station, cross the water, turn right onto Prins Hendrikkade, and left onto Singel. *i* Breakfast included. Free Wi-Fi. ⑤ Singles €60; doubles €95.

Hotel Groenendael   HOTEL $$
Nieuwendijk 15
☎020 624 48 22; www.hotelgroenendael.com

This conveniently located hotel offers some of the cheapest singles in the city. The simple rooms include large windows and a few small terraces.

▶ ⚓ From Centraal Station, turn right, go left at Martelaarsgracht, and turn right onto Nieuwendijk. *i* Breakfast included. Reservations by phone only. Free Wi-Fi. ⑤ Singles €35; doubles €60; triples €90.

SCHEEPVAARTBUURT

Scheepvaartbuurt lacks the stellar hostels of nearby Nieuwe Zijd, but it does have one of the best hotels in the city.

⚐ Frederic Rent-a-Bike
HOTEL $$

Brouwersgracht 78

☎020 624 55 09; www.frederic.nl

Three homey and uniquely decorated rooms, each named after a different artist, sit at the back of Frederic's bike-rental shop. The Mondrian room steals the show with a double **waterbed** and a **hot tub** in the brightly tiled bathroom. Frederic also rents out a number of houseboats and apartments throughout the area. The supremely helpful owners know the city inside-out and will enthusiastically dispense some of the best Amsterdam advice you can find. They also have some great stories to tell; make sure to ask about their experiences with other luminaries of the travel-writing world.

▶ 🚶 From Centraal Station, turn right, cross the Singel, and walk 2 blocks down Brouwersgracht. *i* Breakfast included with hotel rooms. Small rooms have shared bath. Ⓢ Smaller rooms as singles €40-50; as doubles €60-70. Mondrian room €90-100. Houseboats €100-225, with 15% reservation fee.

Hotel My Home
HOTEL $$$

Haarlemmerstraat 82

☎020 624 23 20; www.amsterdambudgethotel.com

This place has been around for a while, as you can tell by their prime piece of internet real estate. The rooms are small and simple, but the yellow walls and patterned bedspreads brighten things up a bit. The relaxed common space includes a pool table. Most rooms are private, but some dorms are available.

▶ 🚶 From Centraal Station, turn right, cross the Singel, and walk down Haarlemmerstraat. *i* Breakfast included (and includes more than toast!). Free Wi-Fi. Ⓢ 5-bed dorms €28-33; Doubles €55-70; triples €84-99; quints €140-165.

Ramenas Hotel
HOTEL $$$

Haarlemmerdijk 61

☎020 624 60 30; www.hotelramenas.nl

Near Haarlemmerplein, Ramenas sits above a cafe of the same name. The rooms are nothing special, but the low ceilings and wooden window frames embrace the cozier side of Amsterdam. Ramenas Hotel isn't a terrible option if more interesting hotels are booked.

▶ 🚶 Tram #3 to Haarlemmerplein. Cross Harlemmerplein to reach Haarlemmerdijk, then continue walking east. Reception is in the cafe downstairs. *i* Breakfast included. Some rooms with bath. Free Wi-Fi. Ⓢ Singles €50-75; doubles €60-100. Additional 5% tourist tax.

CANAL RING WEST

Raadhuisstraat is a row of hotel after hotel, making it a great place to try and find a private room if everywhere else is full. Many hotels are more charming than the busy traffic below might suggest (although almost all have mountainous Amsterdam staircases, so if your grandma is coming along, you might want to spare her). For a quieter and more picturesque location, try one of the accommodations on the **Nine Streets.**

Hotel Clemens   HOTEL $$

Raadhuisstraat 39

☎020 624 60 89; www.clemenshotel.com

Every room in this small hotel is decorated with French-patterned wallpaper and tiered curtains, many revealing great views; some have cushioned window seats, and all have both a fridge and a safe. Enjoy breakfast on the balcony with a view of Westerkerk. Best of all, Hotel Clemens is a great value.

▶ 🚋 Tram #13, 14, or 17 to Westermarkt. Walk across the bridge and it's on the right. *i* Breakfast included. Free Wi-Fi. Ⓢ Singles €40-60; doubles €60-120; triples €120-150.

Nadia Hotel   HOTEL $$$

Raadhuisstraat 51

☎020 620 15 50; www.nadia.nl

Nadia Hotel boasts luxurious rooms with thick red bedspreads, large windows, and built-in wooden shelves. The gorgeous breakfast room is full of hanging plants and a baller view of Westermarkt. The double overlooking the canal will make you feel like you're on a boat. Some deluxe rooms have balconies and views of the canal or Westerkerk. All rooms have desks, coffee and tea makers, safes, and ensuite bathrooms.

▶ 🚋 Tram #13, 14, or 17 to Westermarkt. Walk across the bridge and it will be on your right. *i* Breakfast included. Free Wi-Fi. Computer available. Ⓢ Singles €50-90; doubles €65-100.

Hotel Westertoren   HOTEL $$

Raadhuisstraat 35B

☎020 624 46 39; www.hotelwestertoren.nl

The most exciting room here is the seven-person ensemble, which has two lofted double beds, a single bed underneath, and another double against the opposite wall. Have fun building a fort with your friends—it definitely beats the average hostel. Each room is decorated with traces of the old luxe charm that once characterized this canal house (think red curtains, floral bedspreads, and romantic paintings).

▶ 🚊 Tram #13, 14, or 17 to Westermarkt. Walk across the bridge and it's on the right. *i* Breakfast included, and can be delivered to your room. Free Wi-Fi. All rooms have fridges. Some rooms have balconies. ⓢ Singles €40-60; 7-person room €35 per person (must be booked as a group).

Hotel Pax

HOTEL $$

Raadhuisstraat 37B

☎020 624 97 35; www.hotelpax.nl

The common spaces in Hotel Pax are brightly painted and decorated with mirrors and prints, giving it a much nicer feel than most budget hotels in the neighborhood. The no-frills rooms are outfitted with plain metal-frame beds but are spacious and airy.

▶ 🚊 Tram #13, 14, or 17 to Westermarkt. Cross the bridge and it's on the right. *i* Computer available for a fee. All rooms have cable TV. ⓢ Singles from €35; doubles €60-90; quads €120-150.

Hotel Belga

HOTEL $$

Hartenstraat 8

☎020 624 90 80; www.hotelbelga.nl

Tucked among hip cafes and quirky shops on one of the Nine Streets, this cannabis-friendly hotel remains popular with young travelers. The rooms are large, if a bit plain, but abstract floral paintings brighten up the white walls. Some rooms have slightly slanted floors, which can seem either charming or disorienting depending on your degree of dyspraxia.

▶ 🚊 Tram #13, 14, or 17 to Westermarkt. Cross Keizersgracht, make a right, and then a left onto Hartenstraat. *i* Breakfast included. Free Wi-Fi. ⓢ Singles with shared bath €45-55; doubles €60-100.

Hotel Hegra

HOTEL $$$

Herengracht 269

☎020 623 78 77; www.hotelhegra.nl

Hegra's pretty canal-side location is a bit inconvenient, though it does remove you from the sound of traffic. You'll pay a bit more here than at comparable hotels in the neighborhood. Rooms are clean and simple, with plush red carpeting underfoot and pretty floral tiles.

▶ 🚊 Tram #1, 2, 5, 13, 14, or 17 to Dam. Continue along Raadhuisstraat and make a left onto Herengracht. *i* Breakfast included. Free Wi-Fi. ⓢ Doubles €49-119.

CENTRAL CANAL RING

Stay in the Central Canal Ring if you're looking for private rooms in a relatively quiet atmosphere. You'll still be close to the action of Museumplein, Leidseplein, and Rembrantplein, but you won't have to pay the hefty surcharge that can accompany the short stumbling-distance.

Hemp Hotel   HOTEL $$$
Fredericksplein 15
☎020 625 44 25; www.hemp-hotel.com

Each of Hemp Hotel's rooms has a different geographic theme—the Caribbean, Tibet, and India are all represented—brought to life by hemp fabrics, handmade wood carvings, and vibrant pictures. The Hemple Temple bar downstairs serves a dozen varieties of hemp beer, along with drinks derived from less infamous crops. If you don't mind stained carpets and unpainted wood, it's a great place to hang out and meet chilled-out travelers. Book far in advance—there are a surprising number of travelers who are very excited about showering with hempseed soap and eating hemp rolls for breakfast.

▶ 🚋 Tram #4, 7, 10, or 25 to Fredericksplein. Walk diagonally across the square. *i* Breakfast included. Free Wi-Fi. Ⓢ Singles €60; doubles €70, with bath €75.

The Golden Bear   HOTEL $$$
Kerkstraat 37
☎020 624 47 85; www.goldenbear.nl

Since 1948, this has been Amsterdam's premier gay hotel (about 75% of the guests are male, though women and straight guests are certainly welcome). Besides the fun atmosphere, the hotel is notable for its welcoming staff and well-decorated rooms—if you're lucky, you might get the one with fur on the wall.

▶ 🚋 Tram #1, 2, or 5 to Keizersgracht. Continue down Leidsestraat and turn right. *i* Breakfast included. Free Wi-Fi. Ⓢ Singles with shared bath €65-70; doubles €73-90, with bath €90-130.

Hotel Kap   HOTEL $$
Den Texstraat 5B
☎020 624 59 08; www.kaphotel.nl

Hotel Kap is an especially attractive option in the summer, when you can eat breakfast or relax in the leafy garden out back. The rooms have high ceilings and large windows, though the furnishings are rather plain. It's one of the best deals you'll find in this neighborhood and a good place to look if other hotels are booked, even if the single "student rooms" are a bit cramped.

▶ 🚋 Tram #4, 7, 10, 16, 24, or 25 to Weteringcircuit. Walk down Weteringschans, turn right onto 2e Weteringplantsoen, and left onto Den Texstraat. *i* Breakfast included. All rooms have private showers; singles and some doubles have shared toilet. Wi-Fi €5 per stay. ⓢ Singles €40-65; doubles €60-95.

Hotel Asterisk
HOTEL $$$

Den Texstraat 16

☎020 624 17 68; www.asteriskhotel.nl

Hotel Asterisk offers well-priced rooms in a great location, a pocket of calm between touristy neighborhoods. Rooms with good furniture, pretty paintings, and nice curtains are kept very clean. The simpler twins and singles might feel a little small, but the deluxe rooms with bath are quite spacious.

▶ 🚋 Tram #4, 7, 10, 16, 24, or 25 to Weteringcircuit. Walk down Weteringschans, turn right onto 2e Weteringplantsoen, and left onto Den Texstraat. *i* Breakfast included. Free Wi-Fi. ⓢ Singles €59-68; doubles €60-79, deluxe €89-129.

LEIDSEPLEIN

The best hotels in the Leidseplein are found down **Marnixstraat** and around the bend of the **Leidsekade.**

🏩 Backstage Hotel
HOTEL $$

Leisegracht 114

☎020 624 40 44; www.backstagehotel.com

Popular with musicians in town for shows at nearby clubs, the decor at Backstage adheres to a concert-venue theme: backboards are made to look like trunks, lamps resemble spotlights, lights have drum lampshades, and some rooms have dressing tables that even Lady Gaga would envy. Some suites are quads and quints big enough to house the whole band. Autographed concert posters line the walls and stairways, and reception is accompanied by a bar, pool table, and piano. Open-mic nights are held every Tuesday, and the staff is happy to talk up Amsterdam as well as the hotel's concert schedule. Guitars are available for jamming, and Guitar Hero for pretend jamming.

▶ 🚋 Tram #1, 2, or 5 to Leidseplein. Head away from the sqaure toward Leidsegracht. *i* Most rooms with private bath. Free Wi-Fi. Computer available. ⑤ Singles €35-85; doubles €50-150; quads €150-210; quints €150-250.

Freeland   HOTEL $$$

Marnixstraat 386

☎020 622 75 11; www.hotelfreeland.com

The small, 17-room Freeland feels miles apart from the crowds and grit of the Leidseplein, though the neighborhood's bustling center is just a block away. Rooms are airy and floral, and each one is stocked with amenities like DVD players and coffee makers. Ask if the special double with sunroom is available. Book early, as this place's charm isn't a well-kept secret.

▶ 🚋 Tram #1, 2, 5, 7, or 10 to Leidseplein; or #7 or 10 to Raamplein. *i* Breakfast included. Free Wi-Fi. ⑤ Singles €55-82; doubles €75-125.

International Budget Hostel   HOSTEL $

Leidsegracht 76

☎020 624 27 84; www.internationalbudgethostel.com

This place is popular with students and backpackers, yet still significantly toned down from the Red Light District's party hostels. Maybe things are quieter because everybody is too busy partying outside the hostel in the bars just across the canal. Each dorm has four single beds and lockers. Two private doubles (with shared bath) are also available. The lounge has couches, a TV, and vending machines. Breakfast (€3-8) is served until noon in the canteen.

▶ 🚋 Tram #7 or 10 to Raamplein. Continue walking down Marnixstraat and turn left at the canal. You can also take tram #1, 2, or 5 to Prinsengracht. Turn right and walk along Prinsengracht and then turn left after you cross the bridge. *i* Free Wi-Fi. ⑤ Dorms €20-32.

King Hotel   HOTEL $$$

Leidsekade 85-86

☎020 624 96 03; www.hotel-king.nl

Warmly decorated, impeccably clean rooms with glossy wood and orange curtains fill this hotel, which is located in an old canal house along the bend of the Leidsekade. Some rooms have spectacular views of the water (though you'll pay extra to enjoy them).

▶ 🚋 Tram #1, 2, 5, 7, or 10 to Leidseplein. Walk down Marnixstraat and turn left at the canal; the hotel is around the bend. *i* Breakfast included. Free Wi-Fi. ⑤ Singles €50-75; doubles €75-125.

Hotel Quentin   HOTEL $$
Leidsekade 89
☎020 622 75 11; www.quentinhotels.com

Located in a beautiful renovated mansion overlooking the Leidsekade, this hotel sets itself apart with the funky, abstract furniture and posters of musicians (not to mention flatscreen TVs) that fill its comfortable rooms. The hotel bar serves coffee, alcohol, and soft drinks.

▶ 🚋 Tram #1, 2, 5, 7, or 10 to Leidseplein. Walk down Marnixstraat and turn left at the canal. The hotel is around the bend. *i* Free Wi-Fi. ⑤ Singles €35-55, with bath €40-60; doubles €50-85.

REMBRANDTPLEIN

Rembrandtplein's reputation as a popular nightspot can be both a blessing and a curse. On the one hand, living here means it's easy to stumble home after a long night; on the other, prices and noise levels can be high (especially on weekends).

Hotel the Veteran   HOTEL $$
Herengracht 561
☎020 620 26 73; www.veteran.nl

Hotel the Veteran is a bare-bones establishment, but all the essentials are here. The rooms are clean and cozy with floral bedspreads and wood paneling, which seems to be the go-to tactic for creating welcoming sleeping environments in this city. The hotel sits at the corner of a beautiful stretch of the Herengracht Canal and Thorbeckeplein's strip of bars. Be advised: to enter some rooms you must climb an external staircase next to a bunch of bars, which may be uncomfortable for some travelers returning to their rooms at night. That said, this is one of the cheapest places to stay around Rembrandtplein.

▶ 🚋 Tram #9 or 14 to Rembrandtplein. At the corner of Thorbeckeplein and Herengracht. *i* Breakfast included. Singles all have shared bath; both shared and ensuite doubles available; triples all ensuite. Wi-Fi available. ⑤ Singles €35-65; doubles from €50; triples and family rooms from €65.

City Hotel   HOTEL $$$$
Utrechtstraat 2
☎020 627 23 23; www.city-hotel.nl

City Hotel boasts large, clean rooms, brightly decorated with colorful bedspreads and oversized pictures of flowers. Some rooms have balconies, and those on the top floor have great views of Rembrandtplein and the rest of the city. Many of the rooms are made for five to eight people (some with bunk beds), but none feel cramped. City is popular with groups of young backpackers, since you can find much better values if you're only looking for a double or triple (there are no singles). Breakfast is available—for an extra charge—in a chic dining area with red leather seats.

▶ 🚋 Tram #9 or 14 to Rembrandtplein. City Hotel is off the southeast corner of the main square. *i* Breakfast €7.50. All rooms have safe. Free Wi-Fi and free public computer in dining room. Ⓢ Doubles from €100; triples from €135; 6-person rooms €270.

Hotel Monopole   HOTEL $$$
Amstel 60
☎020 624 62 71

A few blocks removed from the madness of Rembrandtplein, this hotel has simple but pretty pastel rooms, many with canal views (ask ahead). Rooms have the added luxury of breakfast delivered to your door. There's also a cushy common space on the first floor.

▶ 🚋 Tram #9 or 14 to Rembrandtplein. Cut through 1 of the alleyways on the northern side of the square to get to the canal side. *i* Breakfast included. Free Wi-Fi. Ⓢ Singles €65-105; doubles €75-125.

JORDAAN

If you want to live like a local but not commute like one, camp out here.

🏨 Shelter Jordaan   HOSTEL $
Bloemstraat 179
☎020 624 47 17; www.shelter.nl

Smaller and in a quieter location than its sister hostel in the Oude Zijd, the Shelter Jordaan has the same excellent prices, clean facilities, and comfortable atmosphere. They cater to Christian travelers (though all are welcome), so the rooms are single-sex, and drugs and alcohol are forbidden. With speakers blaring an uninterrupted stream of Christian rock, this hostel isn't for everybody, but it's in a good location and feels safe. The rooms are large and bright, with colorful beds and lockers. The large café and garden provide cozy places to hang out and enjoy the free breakfast, which often features pancakes and french toast.

▶ 🚋 Tram #10 to Bloemstraat or tram #13, 14, or 17 to Westermarkt. Follow Lijnbaansgracht for 50m, then turn right onto Bloemstraat. *i* Breakfast included. All rooms with shared bath. Lockers available, though you'll have to bring your own lock or purchase one for €4. Free Wi-Fi. ⓢ 4- to 8-bed dorms €17-30.

Hotel Van Onna   HOTEL $$
Bloemgracht 104
☎020 626 58 01; www.vanonna.nl

The rooms on the top floor of this hotel are truly remarkable, with slanted ceilings, exposed wood beams, and views over the rooftops of the whole Jordaan. You'll need to hike up the stairs to reach them, but at least the staircase is lined with lovely black-and-white photos of the city. The rooms are impeccably clean, though the ones downstairs are dull compared to those upstairs.

▶ 🚋 Tram #10 to Bloemgracht or tram #13, 14, or 17 to Westermarkt. Cross Prinsengracht and turn right; Bloemgracht is 2 blocks away. *i* Breakfast included. Free Wi-Fi. ⓢ Singles €50; doubles €90; triples €135. Credit cards add 5%.

Hotel Acacia   HOTEL $$$
Lindengracht 251
☎020 622 14 60; www.hotelacacia.nl

Tucked in a tranquil corner of the picturesque northern Jordaan, Acacia is nonetheless the epitome of bland and boring. Small studio apartments, which come with a kitchenette and living area, feel a little less institutional.

▶ 🚋 Tram #3 or 10 to Marnixplein. Cross the small canal and make a left onto Lijnbaansgracht; Acacia will be on the right. *i* Breakfast included. All rooms with full bath. Free Wi-Fi. ⓢ Doubles €60-90; studios €70-110.

WESTERPARK AND OUD-WEST

Westerpark is almost exclusively residential with relatively few accommodations. The section of the Oud-West closest to the Leidseplein has a smattering of small hotels, but make sure to bring a good pair of walking shoes or learn how to use the tram if you plan on staying out here. Accommodations cost about the same as their competitors closer to the canal ring, but they are far less crowded and noisy.

Hotel Jupiter   HOTEL $$
2e Helmersstraat 14
☎020 618 71 32; www.jupiterhotel.nl

This hotel sits on one of the small streets parallel to Overtoom, so it's close to transportation and grocery shopping but removed from the bustle and noise of the main thoroughfare. Rooms are sleek and bare, but they're only a 5min. walk from the Leidseplein. Breakfast is included, but the staff can be grouchy.

▶ ✄ Tram #3 or 12 to Overtoom or #1 tp 1e Con. Huygensstraat. Walk 2 blocks away from Vondelpark on 1e Con. Huygensstraat and turn right. ⑤ High-season singles €54, with bath €64; doubles €74/99. Low-season singles €39/49; doubles €59/79. Triples and quads also available.

Hotel Abba   HOTEL $$
Overtoom 116-122
☎020 618 30 58; www.hotel-abba.nl

The rooms here are simple: white walls and gray concrete. This "smoker-friendly" hotel has a very practical location right above an Albert Heijn supermarket. Cable TV (in every room) and breakfast are included. Free safety deposit boxes are available at reception, where the friendly staff will help you arrange trips and tours.

▶ ✄ Tram #1 to 1e Con. Huygensstraat. Above the Albert Heijn. ⑤ High-season singles €50, with bath €60; doubles €70/85. Low-season singles €35/40; doubles €60/70.

MUSEUMPLEIN AND VONDELPARK

You can get your hostel fix without facing the noise and crowds of the Centrum at one of Vondelpark's two excellent backpacker lodgings. Hotels in the neighborhood are removed from the city's best restaurants and bars, but they ooze residential luxury.

🖼 Stayokay Amsterdam Vondelpark   HOSTEL $
Zandpad 5
☎020 589 89 96; www.stayokay.nl/vondelpark

This is a huge hostel—the size makes it feel slightly institutional, but it's clean and well managed. Each room has its own bathroom (the larger rooms have two). Downstairs, an affordable bar with foosball tables, vending machines, and pool tables is a popular hangout. The staff is happy to answer questions about the city, and with so many guests, it won't be hard to find some buddies to venture to nearby Leidseplein with you.

- 🚋 Tram #1, 2, 5, 7, or 10 to Leidseplein. Walk across the canal toward the Marriott, take a left, then make a right onto Zandpad after 1 block. *i* Breakfast included. Single-sex dorms available. Free Wi-Fi. Ⓢ 2- to 20-bed dorms €20-34; singles €50-80.

🏨 Flying Pig Uptown   HOSTEL $
Vossiusstraat 46-47
☎020 400 41 87; www.flyingpig.nl

We find it a little confusing that Flying Pig Uptown is actually south of Flying Pig Downtown (in Nieuwe Zijd), but then again, we can't quite wrap our heads around the fact that the Nile runs south to north... no matter. This is the original Flying Pig, and with a tranquil location across from Vondelpark, this winged swine is a little less rowdy than its younger sibling. Nevertheless, it's still phenomenally popular. The quality of the dorms vary—some are just plain walls and metal-frame bunks—but they're all comfortable and clean, and they each have their own bathrooms. The downstairs boasts a bar with a TV lounge on one side and a smoking room on the other. With proximity to the Leidseplein, guests frequently start off here before going pubbing and clubbing.

- 🚋 Tram #2, 3, 5, or 12 to Van Baerlestraat. Walk down Van Baerlestraat toward Vondelpark and turn right onto Vossiusstraat. *i* Breakfast included. Linens and towel included. Free lockers. Free Wi-Fi. Kitchen available. Ⓢ Dorms €12-40. 🕙 Bar open until 3am.

🏨 Hotel Bema   HOTEL $$
Concertgebouwplein 19B
☎020 679 13 96; www.bemahotel.com

Just across from the stunning Concertgebouw and the major museums on the Museumplein, Hotel Bema boasts elegant rooms with high ceilings, crystal chandeliers, and old-fashioned floral wallpaper. Chambers on the ground floor have antique-style furniture to boot. They'll even deliver breakfast to your room. It's amazing that you can get such luxury at these prices, but no one seems to be arguing with it.

- 🚋 Tram #3, 5, 12, 16, or 24 to Museumplein. Walk down the left side of the Concertgebouw and cross the street. *i* Breakfast included. Free Wi-Fi. Ⓢ Singles €40-45; doubles €65-75, with bath €85-90.

Hotel Museumzicht   HOTEL $$$

Jan Luijkenstraat 22

☎020 671 29 54; www.hotelmuseumzicht.com

Staying here is a bit like staying in your cool grandmother's house—if your grandmother has a perfect view of the Rijksmuseum and serves a traditional Dutch breakfast every day. Old wooden furniture, oriental carpets, and decorative curtains adorn each room. Museumzicht caters to the individual or celibate traveler—there are no double beds, though twins can be pushed together.

▶ ✈ Tram #2 or 5 to Hobbemastraat. Walk away from the Rijksmuseum and turn left onto Jan Luykenstraat. *i* Breakfast included. Free Wi-Fi. Ⓢ Singles €55; doubles €75-85, with bath €85-125.

DE PIJP

Though far from the city center, De Pijp has character and easy transportation options, making it a good place to get a feel for local life in a hip up-and-coming neighborhood.

🏁 Bicycle Hotel   HOTEL $$

Van Ostadestraat 123

☎020 679 34 52; www.bicyclehotel.com

A certain current of yuppie environmentalism runs through De Pijp, so it's appropriate that this eco-conscious hotel is located here. We couldn't be happier: not only does the hotel have solar panels and a "green roof" (plants grow on it and it saves energy—the owners explain it better than we can), but the theme of clean freshness permeates the entire building. The rooms have lavender sheets and pastel prints on the walls, while large windows overlook leafy gardens and let in sun and fresh air. There are even some balconies to sit on. Plus, the per-day bike rental costs the same as a 24hr. transport ticket, so there's no excuse for you not to go green as well.

▶ ✈ Tram #3, 12, or 25 to Ceinturbaan/Ferdinand Bolstraat. Continue 1 block down Ferdinand Bolstraat and turn left onto Van Ostadestraat. *i* Breakfast included. Free Wi-Fi. Ⓢ Singles €35-70; doubles €40-85, with bath €60-120. Bike rental €7.50 per day.

Hotel Vivaldi   HOTEL $$$

Stadhouderskade 76

☎020 577 63 00

Location is everything at this hotel, which sits at the

northern end of the main part of De Pijp, across from the Central Canal Ring. The rooms are minimally furnished (don't worry, there's still a bed), but a few will surprise you with stained-glass windows and great canal views.

▶ 🚋 Tram #16 or 24 to Stadhouderskade. Walk toward the water, veer left, and Hotel Vivaldi is on the left. *i* Breakfast included. Free Wi-Fi. Ⓢ Singles €45-120; doubles €60-150.

JODENBUURT AND PLANTAGE

Staying in these neighborhoods, slightly removed from the city center (though in pocket-sized Amsterdam you're never really far from anything), will give you a more local experience. However, you can expect to pay a little (or a lot) extra for the tranquility.

Bridge Hotel   HOTEL $$$$
Amstel 107-111
☎020 623 70 68; www.thebridgehotel.nl

The nicest hotel in this pricey neighborhood, Bridge's massive, comfortable rooms will easily accommodate you and all the shoes you didn't need to pack. The staff is eager to help you settle into what feels more like a modern Amsterdam apartment than a hotel room (actual apartments with kitchens are also available). The location may feel remote, but you're really just across the bridge from Rembrandtplein.

▶ 🚋 Tram #9 or 14 to Waterlooplein or Mr. Visserplein. Walk down Waterlooplein toward the bridge and turn left onto Amstel. *i* Breakfast included. Free Wi-Fi. Ⓢ Singles €85-115; doubles €98-140.

Hermitage Hotel   HOTEL $$$
Nieuwe Keizersgracht 16
☎020 623 82 59; www.hotelhermitageamsterdam.nl

A new addition to the area, Hermitage has a younger feel than most of the neighboring hotels. Somehow managing to combine two of Amsterdam's predominant hotel aesthetics—modern minimalist and old-fashioned floral—Hermitage covers its walls in stylized silver-and-black flowered wallpaper for a cozy, but urban, feel.

▶ 🚋 Tram #9 or 14 to Waterlooplein or Mr. Visserplein. Walk down Waterlooplein toward the bridge, turn left onto Amstel, and then left onto Nieuwe Keizersgracht. *i* Breakfast €9. Free Wi-Fi. Ⓢ Singles €44-90; doubles €55-120.

Sights

Between the pretty old churches, quaint canals, and nightly showcases of revelry and debauchery, Amsterdam is a sight in and of itself. You can see and learn a lot about the city, even with zero euro. For a little more, you can see Museumplein's excellent art museums (showcasing everything from Northern Renaissance masterpieces to newer avant-garde works), modern photography exhibitions held in hip ex-squat studios and 14th-century churches, and a slew of museums and monuments devoted to remembering WWII. If you're dead set on shunning anything remotely highbrow, there are still plenty of things to see (the Sex Museum and the Hash, Marijuana, and Hemp Museum). Drug-loving tourists shouldn't miss Electric Ladyland, the First Museum of Fluorescent Art—more a trip than a sight, but still highly recommended.

If you're planning on visiting a number of museums, save some euro by investing in the Museumjaarkaart (www.museumjaarkaart.nl). For €40 (or €20 if you're under 26) you get free entrance to most museums in Amsterdam and the Netherlands for a whole year. With the Museumjaarkaart, there's nothing to stop you from popping into one of the many small and weird museums and then popping right back out if it's not up to snuff. You cannot get the card at the tourist office (it's a great deal rarely advertised to tourists), but it's sold at some of the bigger participating museums.

> ### Budget Sights
>
> The Museumjaarkaart is one of the best deals in Amsterdam, and the museum-loving budget traveler should definitely get one (particularly if you're under 26). If you choose to skip it, be careful with the admission fees for Amsterdam's many museums. Ask yourself if you really need to spend €5 to learn the history of the pianola. The city's many free parks let you engage in one of the most entertaining Amsterdam activities: people-watching. And always remember what you're missing when you shell out for overpriced tourist kitsch. Every €5 spent in Amsterdam is €5 that you could have spent at Electric Ladyland.

OUDE ZIJD

While the best museums in Amsterdam are found elsewhere, the Oude Zijd is home to some worthwhile architecture and history. Make some erudite observations on these landmarks on your way to the Red Light District.

Nieuwmarkt   SQUARE

Dominated by the largest still-standing medieval building in Amsterdam, Nieuwmarkt is a calm square lined with cafes and bars, making it one of the best places in the city for some relaxed people-watching. Originally a fortress gate, **De Waag,** the 15th-century castle-like structure in Nieuwmarkt's center, has housed a number of establishments over the years, including a weighing house, a gallery for surgical dissections (Rembrandt's *The Anatomy Lesson of Dr. Tulp* depicts one such event), the **Jewish Historical Museum,** and, today, a swanky restaurant. Nieuwmarkt is beloved by tourists and locals alike: heavy rioting erupted in 1975 in response to a proposal to build a highway through the square. Daily markets here sell everything from souvenirs to organic food, especially on weekends.

▶ ⓂNieuwmarkt, or from Centraal Station walk 10min. down Zeedijk.

Amsterdams Centrum voor Fotografie   GALLERY
Bethanienstraat 39
☎020 622 48 99; www.acf-web.nl

Tucked in a small street between Nieuwmarkt and the Red Light District, this gallery showcases the work of young Dutch photographers, many just out of art school. Exhibits vary greatly in topic and quality, but since it's free, it's worth poking your head in if you're in the neighborhood. The center also holds lectures, workshops, and master classes—all in Dutch.

▶ ✱ ⓂNieuwmarkt. Walk south on Kloveniersburgwal and make a right. ⓢ Free. 🕐 Open Th-Sa 1-5pm.

Oost-Indisch Huis   DUTCH HISTORY
Kloveniersburgwal 48

For almost two centuries, the *Vereenigde Oostindische Compagnie,* or Dutch East India Company—the world's first multinational corporation—wielded quasi-governmental powers and a whole lot of cash. Beginning in 1606, they set up shop in this building along Kloveniersburgwal. Its Dutch Renaissance design is a trademark of Hendrik de Keyser, the architect to whom the building has been (convincingly) attributed. Today, the University of Amsterdam occupies this national monument, and the students loitering and smoking outside take away much of the building's gravitas.

▶ ✱ ⓂNieuwmarkt. Kloveniersburgwal is on the southwestern edge of the sqaure.

RED LIGHT DISTRICT

Many tourists treat the Red Light District as a sight in and of itself, wandering through the crowded streets while pretending not to look at window prostitutes. But there are plenty of other worthwhile opportunities for travelers to learn about parts of Dutch history and culture that don't involve sex, drugs, and drunk frat boys.

🖼 Oude Kerk   CHURCH
Oudekerksplein 23

☎020 625 82 84; www.oudekerk.nl

Since its construction in 1306, Oude Kerk, the oldest church in Amsterdam, has endured everything from the Protestant Reformation to the growth of the Red Light District, which today encroaches naughtily on its very square. (Case in point: the bronze relief of a hand caressing a breast set into the cobblestones outside.) Oude Kerk didn't escape all this history unscathed; during the Reformation of 1578, the church lost much of its artwork and religious figures. However, it remains a strikingly beautiful structure, with massive vaulted ceilings and gorgeous stained glass that betray the building's Catholic roots. You can occasionally hear concerts played on

> ### Subprime Tulip Crisis
>
> What can tulips tell us about the current global financial situation? A lot, actually. In 1593, tulips were brought from Turkey to the Netherlands, where they soon contracted the "mosaic" virus, which caused flames of color to develop on the petals. The colorful flowers became increasingly desirable, and, in just one month, tulips increased 20 times in value. At the height of tulip mania, you could trade a single tulip for an entire estate. Pubs turned into tulip exchanges at night, and people from all social strata staked their homes and livelihoods on the precious bulbs in a frenzy of what the Dutch call *windhandel,* or "trading in the wind"—speculating without any actual goods to back it up.
>
> When the market inevitably crashed overnight in 1637, prices took a nosedive. A tulip was suddenly worth no more than an onion. The whole credit system fell apart and the Netherlands experienced a major depression whose reverberations were felt across Europe.
>
> Today, Amsterdam hosts tours about tulip mania. Bankers and investors could definitely learn a thing or two from these pretty, but financially deadly, flowers.

the grandiose **Vater-Muller organ,** which dates back to 1724, but Oude Kerk is now used mainly for art and photography exhibitions, including the display of the prestigious **World Press Photo** prizewinners. Whether you come for the art, music, or the sanctuary, tread lightly—you're walking on 35 generations of Amsterdam's dead.

▶ ✯ From Centraal Station, walk down Damrak, turn left onto Oudebrugsteeg, and right onto Warmoesstraat; the next left leads to the church. *i* Check the website for a calendar of performances. ⑤ €7.50; students, seniors, and under 13 €5.50; with Museumjaarkaart free. ⌚ Open M-Sa 10am-5:30pm, Su 1-5:30pm.

▨ Ons' Lieve Heer op Solder   MUSEUM
Oudezijds Voorburgwal 40
☎020 624 66 04; www.opsolder.nl

The Ons' Lieve Heer op Solder ("Our Lord in the Attic") museum commemorates a beautiful Catholic church... in an attic. Built by a merchant in the 17th century, when Catholicism was officially banned in the Netherlands, the church was once regularly packed with secret worshippers. The museum includes three houses whose connected offices house the church, featuring art and furniture from the period. In contrast to the Catholic lavishness of Oude Kerk around the corner, Ons' Lieve Heer op Solder highlights the more muted Catholicism of the post-Reformation era. The church contains an impressive organ and a beautiful altarpiece by the famous painter **Jacob de Wit,** but the real appeal is the understanding you'll gain of broader trends in Dutch history and culture.

▶ From Centraal Station, turn left onto Prins Hendrikkade and then right onto Nieuwebrugsteeg. Continue straight as Nieuwebrugsteeg becomes Oudezijds Voorburgwal. ⑤ €7, students €5, under 18 €1, under 5 and with Museumjaarkaart free. Open M-Sa 10am-5pm, Su 1-5pm.

Brouwerij de Prael BREWERY

Oudezijds Voorburgwal 30
☎020 408 44 70; www.deprael.nl

If you love beer but find yourself asking "what's a hops?" come get a quick and easy crash course with a tour of this favorite local brewery. All the beer is organic, unfiltered, and unpasteurized, and all are named after classic *levensliederen,* sappy Dutch love songs (aww). A brewery that does more than make beer, de Prael was founded by two former psychiatrists and now employs over 60 people with a history of mental illness. The attached store sells de Prael's beers and other merchandise.

▶ From Centraal Station, turn left onto Prins Hendrikkade and then right onto Nieuwebrugsteeg. Continue straight as it becomes Oudezijds Voorburgwal. ⑤ Tour with 1 beer €7.50, with tasting menu €16.50. Brewery open M-F 9am-5pm. Tasting room open Tu-Su 11am-11pm.

Cannabis College MUSEUM

Oudezijds Achterburgwal 124
☎020 423 44 20; www.cannabiscollege.com

Get your druggie "diploma" (a bachelor's in blunts? a master's in marijuana? a doctorate in doobies?) by taking a short quiz on all things cannabis. If you want cold, hard, sticky-icky facts, this is a repository of any information you could ever want to know about hemp and marijuana, especially regarding growing the plants themselves. Friendly volunteers, who are knowledgeable enough to provide training workshops to coffeeshop owners, are happy to answer questions about the history, science, and use of the drug. If you're dying to see some of the plants in person, check out the garden downstairs—otherwise, save the couple of euro and check out the pictures on their website. If you're looking for more kitsch, try the **Hash Marijuana Hemp Museum** just a few doors down (Oudezijds Achterburgwal 148; www.hashmuseum.com ⑤ €9).

▶ ⁂ From Dam Sq., walk east on Dam and make a left onto Oudezijds Achterburgwal. ⑤ Free. Garden €2.50. ⏲ Open daily 11am-7pm.

NIEUWE ZIJD

The Nieuwe Zijd (despite its name) is one of the oldest parts of the city. Go back in time at the Amsterdam Historical Museum, then get a rude awakening into the present at some of the area's gimmicky attractions, such as Madame Tussaud's and the Sex Museum.

Nieuwe Kerk   CHURCH, MUSEUM
Dam Sq.

☎020 638 69 09; www.nieuwekerk.nl

Built in 1408 when the Oude Kerk became too small for the city's growing population, the Nieuwe Kerk is a commanding Gothic building that holds its own amid the architectural extravaganza of Dam Sq. Inside, the church is all vaulted ceilings and massive windows. Don't miss the intricate organ case designed by Jacob van Campen, architect of the Koninklijk Palace. Today, the Nieuwe Kerk is the site of royal inaugurations (the most recent one being Queen Beatrix's in 1980) and some royal weddings (like Prince Willem-Alexander's in 2002). Most of the year, however, the space serves as a museum. Each winter, the church holds exhibits on foreign cultures, specifically focusing on world religions (recent topics have included Islam and Ancient Egypt). The space is also used for temporary exhibits by prominent Dutch museums like the Stedelijk and Rijksmuseum. Organ concerts are held here every Sunday, while shorter and more informal organ recitals are performed on Thursday afternoons.

▶ ⁂ Any tram to Dam Sq. Nieuwe Kerk is on the northeastern edge of the square. ⑤ €5, students €4, with Museumjaarkaart free. Organ concerts €8.50; recitals €5. ⏲ Open daily 10am-5pm. Recitals Th 12:30pm. Concerts Su 8pm.

Amsterdam Sex Museum   MUSEUM
Damrak 18

☎020 622 83 76; www.sexmuseumamsterdam.nl

Unless you were previously unaware that people have been

having sex since mankind's origin, there's not much new information about sex or sexuality in this museum. (The brief "Sex Through the Ages" presentation is hilariously simplistic, though the elegant British-accented narration is priceless.) But let's face it: who needs information when you've got smut? Tons of pornographic photographs, paintings, and life-sized dolls fill the museum, along with models of various sexual icons: Marilyn Monroe with her skirt fluttering over the subway vent, a 1980s pimp, and even a **flasher** who thrills the audience every few seconds. The museum attracts crowds of tourists who react quite differently: some leave slightly offended by the hardcore porn-and-fetish room, some find the farting dolls funny, and others inexplicably insist on having their picture taken with one of the giant model penises. If you really want to see a parade of pictures of people having sex, you could just visit a sex shop in the Red Light District, but at least the Sex Museum charges a low rate for its high kitsch factor. Be warned: after you see (and hear) the mannequins of a Dutch girl giving a handjob in a public urinal, you may never look at one of those Dutch "curlies" the same way again.

▶ From Centraal Station, walk straight down Damrak. *i* 16+. €4. Open daily 9:30am-11:30pm.

Amsterdam Historical Museum MUSEUM
Nieuwezijds Voorburgwal 359
☎020 523 18 22; www.amsterdammuseum.nl

People, schmeople. This museum is about Amsterdam as a city. Through paintings, artifacts, and multimedia presentations, the museum's "Grand Tour" will show you how Amsterdam changed from 1350 to the present (spoiler: it changed a lot). Don't miss the room dedicated to Golden Age art and its stomach-churning paintings of anatomy lessons, which were apparently all the rage in the 17th century. Also fascinating is the corner that shows various city planning designs from the past century, driving home the fact that Amsterdam is an entirely man-made city. Only true history buffs will really be intrigued enough to read the placards about mercantile ships, but accessible and interesting temporary exhibits make up for some of the slower material. If you want to get to know the city a little better, this is a great place to start.

▶ Tram #1, 2, or 5 to Spui/Nieuwezijds Voorburgwal. Head up Nieuwezijds Voorburgwal and the museum is on the right. €10, seniors €7.50, students and ages 6-18 €5, under 6 and with Museumjaarkaart free. Audio tour €4.50. ☼ Open M-F 10am-5pm, Sa-Su 11am-5pm.

Begijnhof
COURTYARD, CHURCH

Begijnhof
www.begijnhofamsterdam.nl

The Beguines were small groups of Catholic laywomen who took vows of chastity and chose to serve the Church, though they didn't retreat from the world and formally join a convent. After seeing this beautiful 14th-century courtyard, surrounded by the Beguines' homes, you'll agree that they made a good call: this is a pretty sweet crib. Tour groups, bicycles, and photographs aren't allowed, so take in the place's original tranquility. During the Alteration, the original chapel was turned into a Protestant place of worship. The women responded by using a secret Catholic church, the **Begijnhofkapel**, built within two of the houses. Today, the cute but unremarkable chapel is an English Presbyterian church (the Belgians would be livid) and is open to respectful visitors.

▶ 🚋 Tram #1, 2, or 5 to Spui/Nieuwezijds Voorburgwal. Walk down Gedempte Begijnsloot and the gardens are on the left. ⑤ Free. ☼ Open daily 9am-5pm.

Dam Square
SQUARE

Once upon a time, Amsterdam was just two small settlements on either side of the Amstel River. One day the villagers decided to connect their encampments with a dam. Since then, Dam Sq. has been the heart of the city, home to markets, the town hall, a church, and a weigh house (until Napoleon's brother had it torn down because it blocked his view). The obelisk on one end is the **Nationaal Monument,** erected in 1956 to honor the Dutch victims of WWII. The wall surrounding the monument contains soil from cemeteries and execution sites in each of the Netherlands's 12 provinces, as well as the Dutch East Indies. Across from the monument, next to the Nieuwe Kerk, you'll find the **Koninklijk Palace** (www.paleisamsterdam.nl), where you can see what it's like to be Dutch royalty. Louis Napoleon took it over in 1808, deciding that the building (constructed in the 17th century as Amsterdam's town hall) would make an excellent fixer-upper. Since then, it has been a royal palace, although Queen Beatrix only uses it for official functions.

Too bad—she's wasting a unique view of the crowds, street performers, and occasional concerts in the square below.

▶ 🚋 Tram #1, 2, 4, 5, 9, 13, 14, 16, 17, 24, or 25 to Dam (remember when we said this was the center of the city?). 💲 Palace €7.50; ages 5-16, over 65, and students €6.50; with Museumjaarkaart free. ⏰ Palace usually open noon-5pm; check website for details.

CANAL RING WEST

The Canal Ring West is home to a few must-see sights (the Anne Frank House and nearby Westerkerk should be near the top of your list) along with some wackier ones like the Nationaal Brilmuseum and the National Spectacles Museum (Gasthuismolensteeg; www.brilmuseumamsterdam.nl).

🏛 Anne Frank House   MUSEUM

Prinsengracht 267

☎020 556 71 00; www.annefrank.nl

This is one of the most frequently visited sights in the city, and for good reason. It is the house where Anne Frank and her family lived in hiding from 1942 to 1944, when they were finally arrested by the Nazis. The well-organized museum route takes you through the family's hiding place, starting behind the moveable bookcase that masked their secret annex. Displays include pages of Anne's famous diary and a model of the rooms in 1942—Anne's father Otto requested that the museum not re-furnish the actual annex rooms after the Nazis seized all the original furnishings. Videos featuring interviews with those who knew the family make the story even more tangible. The end of the route includes information and interactive displays on contemporary issues in human rights and discrimination, reflecting the museum's mission as a center for activism and education as well as remembrance. This is one of the few museums in Amsterdam that opens early and stays open late, and we recommend you take advantage of it: the cramped attic gets packed with visitors in the middle of the day, and you'll want to be able to move around and take your time in such a thought-provoking place.

▶ 🚋 Tram #13, 14, or 17 to Westermarkt. Walk away from Keizersgracht down Westermarkt, then take a right onto Prinsengradcht. 💲 €8.50, ages 10-17 €4, under 10 and with Museumjaarkaart free. ⏰ Open daily July-Aug 9am-10pm; Sept 1-14 9am-9pm; Sept 15-March 14 9am-7pm; March 15-June 9am-9pm.

Westerkerk   CHURCH
Prinsengracht 281

☎020 624 77 66; www.westerkerk.nl

Westerkerk's 85m tower, the Westerkerkstoren, stands far above central Amsterdam's other buildings. A trip up it in a 30min. guided tour is a must. The patient staff will pause to accommodate your huffing and puffing until you finish the climb and step out to behold the best view in Amsterdam. The tower also houses 47 bells, one of which weighs in at an astonishing 7509kg. The church was completed in 1631, a gift to the city from Maximilian of Austria (whose crown can be seen on the tower) in thanks for the city's support of the Austro-Burgundian princes. The church's brick-and-stone exterior is a fine example of Dutch late-Renaissance architecture. Inside, its plain white walls and clear glass windows are typical of the clean Calvinist aesthetic. The only real decorations are the shutters on the organ, which are beautifully painted by Gerard de Lairesse. The tower's carillon plays between noon and 1pm on Tuesdays, free organ concerts are held every Friday at 1pm, and the church hosts many other concerts throughout the year. Queen Beatrix and Prince Claus were married here in 1966, and Rembrandt is buried somewhere within the church—although no one seems to know exactly where. (Yeah, we don't know how they forgot where they put one of the most famous painters of all time either.)

▶ 🚋 Tram #13, 14, or 17 to Westermarkt. Walk away from Keizersgracht and turn right onto Prinsengradcht. Ⓢ Free. Tower tour €7. 🕐 Open Apr-June M-F 10am-6pm, Sa 10am-8pm; July-Sept M-Sa 10am-8pm; Oct M-F 11am-4pm, Sa 10am-6pm. Tower tours every 30min.

Homomonument   MONUMENT
Westermarkt

www.homomonument.nl

The Homomonument is the culmination of a movement to erect a memorial honoring homosexual victims of Nazi persecution, but it's also meant to stand for all people, past and present, who've been oppressed for their sexuality. Designed by Karin Daan and officially opened in 1987, the monument consists of three pink granite triangles (in remembrance of the symbol the Nazis forced homosexuals to wear), connected by thin lines of pink granite to form a larger triangle. The Homomonument was designed to merge seamlessly with the daily life of the city, so it can be hard to discern under picnicking tourists and whizzing bikes. One triangle is set down into

Poezenboot

At first, Henriette van Weelde was your typical cat lady. In 1966, she took in a family of stray cats she found across from her home. Then she took in another. And another. After a while, she realized she had a bit of a space issue—namely, too many cats, too little space. So, Henriette did the reasonable thing: she bought her feline friends a sailing barge. The cats never stopped coming, so she upgraded the boat a few times over the years. By 1987, the boat was named an official cat sanctuary. Today, it meets all the requirements for an animal shelter. The Poezenboot (Cat Boat) has room for 30 kitties, and they adopt out an average of 15 per month. If you find yourself looking for a different kind of pussy in Amsterdam, stop by to offer one a good home. (Singel 38G ☎020 625 87 94; www.poezenboot.nl ◯ Open M-Tu 1-3pm, Th-Sa 1-3pm.)

---

the water of the Keizergracht and points toward the National War Monument in Dam Sq., representing the present. The raised triangle stands for the future and points toward the headquarters of the COC, a Dutch gay rights group founded in 1946 and the oldest continuously operating gay and lesbian organization in the world. The third triangle points toward the Anne Frank House, symbolizing the past; it is engraved with the words *"Naar Vriendschap Zulk een Mateloos Verlangen"* ("such an endless desire for friendship"), a line from the poem "To a Young Fisherman" by the gay Dutch Jewish poet Jacob Israel de Haan (1881-1924).

▶ ☤ Tram #13, 14, or 17 to Westermarkt. The Homomonument is between Westerkerk and the Keizersgracht. ⓢ Free.

Multatuli Museum   MUSEUM
Korsjespoortsteeg 20
☎020 638 19 38; www.multatuli-museum.nl

This museum is dedicated to the Netherlands's most famous writer, Eduard Douwes Dekker, who was born here in 1820. Dekker was better known by his pen name, Multatuli—Latin for "I have endured much." He was a rather unsuccessful lad, and after failing at school and a trade clerkship, he was carted off to Indonesia by his sea captain father. Here, he finally exhibited some talent in the civil service, rising through the ranks and marrying a baroness along the way. Disgusted by the abuses of imperialism, he eventually quit his job, returned to a penniless life in Europe, and wrote the autobiographical novel *Max Havelaar* to expose the evils of colonialism and the Dutch East India Company. Ironically, *Max Havelaar* became a massive hit, not due to its message of reform (which was largely ignored by the contemporary public) but because of Multatuli's entertaining, well-written prose. In time, the work came to be cited as one of the most important books to influence reform movements. Today, *Max Havelaar* remains the most popular Dutch novel, and has been translated into more than 40 languages. Multatuli is considered a crucial intellectual forefather to the atmosphere of tolerance for which the Netherlands is so famous today.

The dedicated proprietor of the museum, who cares passionately about Multatuli's legacy, will gladly tell you everything about the author's life in the form of personal and funny stories. The free museum is worth a stop for literary fiends, those who want a quick brush-up on Dutch history, or those curious to learn more about the brain inside the enormous head replicated in the big statue over the Singel.

▶ ⚡ Tram #1, 2, 5, 13, or 17 to Nieuwezijds Kolk. Walk to the Herengracht and make a right. ⓢ Free (but don't forget to tip the guide!). ⓓ Open Tu 10am-5pm, Sa-Su 10am-5pm.

Nederlands Instituut voor Mediakunst   MUSEUM
Keizersgracht 264
☎020 623 71 01; www.nimk.nl

The Netherlands Media Art Institute puts on four 10-week exhibitions each year to showcase the works of Dutch and international artists who use film, video, the internet, and other media technology. If you're planning a visit, be prepared to invest some time, as pieces can sometimes run for 20min. or more, but most are interesting enough that you'll want to see the whole thing. The institute also runs a number of smaller exhibitions that involve more experimental performances and symposia. The museum is in the same building as the **Mediatheque,** which houses a huge collection of books and media pieces.

▶ ⚡ Tram #13, 14, or 17 to Westermarkt. Follow Keizersgracht and the museum will be on your right. ⓢ €4.50, students and seniors €2.50. Mediatheque free. ⓓ Open Tu-F 11am-6pm, Sa and every 1st Su 1-6pm. Mediatheque open M-F 1-5pm.

Bijbels Museum
MUSEUM

Herengracht 366-368

☎020 624 24 36; www.bijbelsmuseum.nl

This bizarre museum provides glimpses into two radically different worlds: ancient biblical culture and 17th-century Dutch life. The centerpiece is the Tabernacle model, the life work of minister Leendert Schouten (1828-1905), who based the original museum around public Tabernacle viewings. The top floor has Egyptian artifacts—sculptures, sarcophagi, even a mummy—that are meant to illustrate the Israelite presence in Egypt. Some exhibits also deal with the history of Islam and Judaism. The ground floor shows artifacts of 17th-century domestic life. Adjacent are two reading rooms and the somewhat perplexing **Aroma Room,** which has samples of biblical scents like cedar and myrrh free for the sniffing.

▶ 🚋 Tram #1, 2, or 5 to Koningsplein. Walk down Koningsplein toward the bridge, then make a right onto Herengracht. ⓢ €8, students €4.75, ages 13-17 €4, with Museumjaarkart free. ⓘ Open M-Sa 10am-5pm, Su 11am-5pm.

CENTRAL CANAL RING

The grand buildings in the center of the canal ring, architectural landmarks themselves, house a few historical museums as well as art galleries that lean toward the avant-garde. For kitsch aficionados, come here for some of the quirkier museums in the city, like the **Cat's Cabinet** (see below) or the **Museum of Bags and Purses** (Herengracht 573 ☎020 524 64 52; http://www.tassenmuseum.nl).

🖼 FOAM
MUSEUM

Keizersgracht 609

☎020 551 65 00; www.foam.org

Foam—the **Fo**tografiemuseum **Am**sterdam—showcases new photography, from gritty photojournalism to glossy fashion photos. Work by renowned and up-and-coming photographers is displayed in an expansive wood-and-metal space. Grab a coffee and try to blend in with the artsy students hanging out here.

▶ 🚋 Tram #4, 16, 24, or 25 to Keizersgracht. Foam is about 50m east of the stop. ⓢ €8, students and seniors €5.50, under 12 and with Museumjaarkaart free. ⓘ Open M-W 10am-6pm, Th-F 10am-9pm, Sa-Su 10am-6pm. Cafe open daily 11am-5pm.

Golden Bend ARCHITECTURE
Herengracht, between Leidsestraat and Vijzelstraat

If Amsterdam's tiny, teetering canal houses are beginning to make you feel claustrophobic, head to this scenic stretch of the canal ring, removed from the noisy center but still only 15min. south of Dam Sq. In the 17th century, expanding the canals meant the city needed wads of cash, so they allowed the rich to build houses twice as wide as before in order to encourage investment. Termed the "Golden Bend" for the wealth that subsequently flocked here, this stretch of former residences features Neoclassical facades and glimpses of sparkling chandeliers through latticed windows. Today, most of these former mansions are inhabited by banks, life insurance agencies, and a few very lucky (and very wealthy) residents. To get a peek inside one of the swanky buildings, you may have to stifle your suppressed fear of crazy cat ladies and visit **Cat's Cabinet** (Herengracht 497 ☎020 626 53 78; www.kattenkabinet.nl). This bizarre museum was created a Golden Bend house after the owner's beloved cat—fittingly named JP Morgan—passed away. For some reason, the apparently distraught owner felt the world needed a museum devoted to all things feline. For a less idiosyncratic peek inside, **Open Garden Days** each June allow visitors to tour many of the houses' gardens (for more info, check out www.opentuinendagen.nl).

▶ ✇ Tram #1, 2, or 5 to Koningsplein. ⑤ Cat's Cabinet €6, ages 4-12 €3. ⌚ Cat's Cabinet open M-F 10am-4pm, Sa-Su noon-5pm.

Museum Willet-Holthuysen MUSEUM
Herengracht 605
☎020 523 18 22; www.willetholthuysen.nl

Not technically on the "Golden Bend" but just as elegant and opulent, this building has been preserved by the Amsterdam Historical Museum. The museum's goal is to demonstrate what wealthy Dutch life was like in the 19th century as seen through the eyes of **Abraham Willet** and **Louisa Willet-Holthuysen,** the house's last inhabitants. Visitors gawk and admire three floors of wealth on display, including the Willets' art collection and a stately garden. Those less interested in history might tire of all the tidbits from the meticulously chronicled lives of Louisa and Abe, but if you've got a few minutes and a Musuemjaarkaart, the inside offers a new perspective on the famous canal houses. The museum will leave you wondering if all the tall skinny abodes you trek past are this ridiculously grand.

▶ 🚊 Tram #9 or 14 to Rembrandtplein. Walk down Utrechtsestraat and turn left. ⓢ €8, ages 6-18 €4, under 6 and with Museumjaarkaart free. 🕐 Open M-F 10am-5pm, Sa-Su 11am-5pm.

JORDAAN

The Jordaan is home to some of Amsterdam's quirkiest sights. Those uninterested in the psychedelic trip that is **Electric Ladyland** can visit the **Pianola Museum,** dedicated to self-playing pianos. Even if you just pass through, look for the **Hofjes,** and some of the most beautiful canal views in the city.

🖼 Electric Ladyland   MUSEUM
Tweede Leliedwarsstraat 5
☎020 420 37 76; www.electric-lady-land.com

Electric Ladyland, the "First Museum of Fluorescent Art," is a sight unlike any other. The passionate and eccentric owner, Nick Padalino, will happily spend hours explaining the history, science, and culture of fluorescence to each and every visitor who walks through the door. The museum consists of a one-room basement full of Padalino's own art and other artifacts, including rocks and minerals from New Jersey to the Himalayas that glow all kinds of colors under the lights. The most intriguing part though, is the fluorescent cave-like sculpture that Padalino terms "participatory art." Don a pair of foam slippers and poke around the glowing grottoes and stalactites; flick the lights on and off to see different fluorescent and phosphorescent stones; and look for the tiny, hidden Hindu sculptures. Upstairs, you can buy your own fluorescent art and blacklight kits. When a tour is in progress, you may have to ring the doorbell for a few minutes, but trust us: it's worth any wait.

▶ 🚊 Tram #13, 14, or 17 to Westermarkt. Cross Prinsengracht and walk 1 block down Rozengracht, then make a right and walk a few blocks. The museum is just before you reach Egelantiersgracht. ⓢ €5. 🕐 Open Tu-Sa 1-6pm.

Stedelijk Museum Bureau Amsterdam (SMBA)   MUSEUM
Rozenstraat 59
☎020 422 04 71; www.smba.nl

There's no telling what you'll find at the Stedelijk Museum's project space, but it seems to usually be some kind of art. Local artists have the chance to showcase artwork in rotating exhibits; during *Let's Go*'s last visit it was "The Marx Lounge"—a red room with a table full of books on critical theory. Special lectures and movie screenings are also sponsored occasionally. Check the website for current events or simply take your chances and drop by—after all, it's free.

▶ ⚡ Tram #13, 14, or 17 to Westermarkt. Cross Prinsengracht, turn left, and walk 1 block. ⓢ Free. ☼ Open Tu-Su 11am-5pm.

Hofjes
GARDENS, DUTCH HISTORY

The northern third of the Jordaan

Tucked behind the neighborhood's closed doors are some of the oldest and prettiest gardens in the city. *Hofjes* are courtyard gardens, surrounded by almshouses originally built to provide housing for impoverished old women. These old gardens are scattered throughout the Jordaan, and many are now open to the public. In the northern part of the Jordaan, at Palmgracht 28-38, you can find the **Raepenhofje,** and a few blocks down is the **Karthuizerhof** (Karthuizersstraat 21-131). This larger *hofje* has two flowering gardens dotted with benches and a pair of old-fashioned water pumps. Finally, head to Egelantiersgracht 107-145 for the **Sint-Andrieshof.** These gardens are surrounded by residences, so be quiet and respectful.

▶ ⚡ From Raepenhofje, take tram #3 to Nieuwe Willemstraat, cross Lijnbaansgracht, make a left, and turn right onto Palmgracht. ⓢ Free. ☼ Open M-Sa 9am-6pm.

WESTERPARK AND OUD-WEST

Visitors to this area can relax in the park that gives the neighborhood its name, while art-lovers could check out two of the city's more idiosyncratic destinations, to the north and east of the park.

Museum Het Schip
MUSEUM

Spaarndammerplantsoen 140

☎020 418 28 85; www.hetschip.nl

This museum commemorates "The Ship," a housing project designed by Amsterdam School architect Michel de Klerk in 1919. Inspired by Socialist ambitions, de Klerk added unusual shapes and fanciful brickwork to his building, believing that Amsterdam's working class was overdue for "something beautiful." The first floor houses an old post office designed by de Klerk, as well as a re-creation of what one of the original apartments looked like. Be sure to take the free tour, as knowledgeable staff can point out quirky details in the architecture that are otherwise easily missed. Across the street, a lunchroom serves food amid an exhibit of Amsterdam School photography and sculptures.

▶ ⁂ Tram #3 to Haarlemmerplein. Walk across the canal toward Westerpark, up Spaarndammerstraat, then take a left onto Zaanstraat; the building will be a few blocks down the street. ⓢ €7.50, students €5, with Museumjaarkaart free. ⓘ Open Tu-Su 11am-5pm. Tours every hr. 11am-4pm, though they can usually be joined late.

Westergasfabriek   CULTURAL PARK
Pazzanistraat 41
☎020 586 07 10; www.westergasfabriek.nl

Westergasfabriek, a so-called "cultural park" right next to Westerpark, serves as a center for local artists and trendy restaurants. Originally a 19th-century gasworks, its imposing brick buildings are now open to all manner of cultural projects, and currently house art studios and galleries, restaurants, theaters, and nightclubs. Check the website for upcoming showings and special events like film festivals, art showings, and market days.

▶ ⁂ Just east of Westerpark. Tram #10 to Van Hallstraat. Cross the bridge and turn right to get to the main cluster of buildings.

MUSEUMPLEIN AND VONDELPARK

The Museumplein is filled with museums—surprise! Plus, the beautiful **Concertgebouw,** at the southern end of Museumplein, is worth checking out even when the music isn't playing (see **Arts and Culture**).

▧ Van Gogh Museum   MUSEUM
Paulus Potterstraat 7
☎020 570 52 00; www.vangoghmuseum.nl

Van Gogh only painted for about a decade, yet he left a remarkable legacy of paintings and drawings. There's a lot more here than the pictures on the walls: one exhibit has a graphic novel depicting van Gogh's tumultuous personal life, while another details how the paintings have changed over the years with recreations of the masterpieces as the painter himself would've seen them. The museum dedicates considerable space to the artists who influenced van Gogh; including Toulouse-Lautrec, Gauguin, Renoir, Manet, Seurat, and Pissarro. On the flip side there are some paintings influenced by van Gogh, from artists like Derain and Picasso. Of course, the highlight of the museum is its impressive collection of van Gogh's own work—the largest in the world—ranging from the dark, gloomy works like the *Potato Eaters* and *Skull of a Skeleton with Burning Cigarette* to the delicate *Branches of an Almond Tree in Blossom*. The exhibits are arranged chronologically, and wall plaques do an excellent job tracking the artist's biography alongside the paintings, concluding with the artist's descent into depression and suicide. We think this may be the best museum in Amsterdam—unfortunately, so do a lot of other people. The lines can get pretty painful; to avoid them, reserve tickets on the museum's website or arrive when the crowds thin at around 10:30am or 4pm. But don't let the fear of crowds deter you—this is hands down one of the city's must-sees, and it's absolutely worth the wait.

▶ ⌘ Tram #2, 3, 5, or 12 to Van Baerlestraat. Walk 1 block up Paulus Potterstraat. ⓢ €14, under 18 and with Museumjaarkaart free. Audio tour €5. ⓘ Open M-Th 10am-6pm, F 10am-10pm, Sa-Su 10am-6pm. Last entry 30 min. before close.

▩ Rijksmuseum   MUSEUM
Jan Luijkenstraat 1
☎020 674 70 00; www.rijksmuseum.nl

When you first see the commanding facade of the Rijksmuseum, it looks like the type of place you could get lost in for hours (if not days). Luckily—if a bit disappointingly—the museum is undergoing extensive renovations (scheduled to be completed in 2013), so only highlights of the collection are currently on display. It's still well worth a visit, though. Current displays feature art and artifacts from the Middle Ages through the 19th century, a comprehensive exhibit on Dutch history, and a collection of Asian art. There is also an enormous selection of furniture, Delftware, silver, and decorative objects (including two enormous dollhouses that probably cost more than some apartments). The exhibits on the ground floor trace the Netherlands's history as it grew from a small republic to a world power, commanding more than a fair share of the seas and international trade. The heart of the museum, however, is the second-floor gallery of art from the Dutch Golden Age. Numerous still lifes—cheese figures prominently, typical Dutch—landscapes, and portraits set the tone for 17th-century Dutch art, reflecting the same trends as the history lesson on the first floor. They pull out the big guns in a room full of beautiful works by **Rembrandt** and his pupils, evocative landscapes by Jacob van Ruisdael, and four luminous paintings by **Vermeer,** including *The Milkmaid.* The big finish is the room devoted to the **Night Watch,** probably Rembrandt's most famous painting. Only in Amsterdam would the old master be exhibited alongside a modern sculpture that looks like metal magic mushrooms hanging upside-down. Two audio tours are available to guide you through the museum. One is more traditional and led by the museum director, while the other is narrated by the Dutch artist, actor, and director Jeroen Krabbé, who gives a more personal view of the artists and paintings.

▶ 🚋 Tram #2 or 5 to Hobbemastraat. Alternatively, tram #7 or 10 to Spiegelgracht. The museum is directly across the canal. *i* Lines are shorter after 4pm. ⑤ €12.50, under 18 and with Museumjaarkaart free. Audio tour €5. ⓘ Open daily 9am-6pm.

Vondelpark   PARK

Rolling streams, leafy trees, and inviting grass make the 120-acre Vondelpark central Amsterdam's largest and most popular open space. Established in the 1880s to provide a place for the city's residents to walk and ride, the park is now a hangout for skaters, senior citizens, stoners, soccer players, and sidewalk acrobats. Head here on the first sunny day of spring to see the whole city out in full force. The park is named after Joost van den Vondel, a 17th-century poet and playwright often referred to as the "Dutch Shakespeare." Vondelpark is also home to excellent cafes and an open-air theater (www.openluchttheater.nl), which offers free music and performances in the summer. If you're looking for a different sort of outdoor entertainment, you should know that in 2008 the Dutch police decided that it's legal to **have sex** in Vondelpark—so long as it's not near a playground and condoms are thrown away. Even without a bit of afternoon delight, this is still a delightful place to picnic and take a break from the bustling city.

▶ 🚋 Tram #2, 3, 5, or 12 to Van Baerlestraat. Walk down Van Baerlestraat to the bridge over the park and take the stairs down.

DE PIJP

De Pijp's sights are of a decidedly different variety than those in nearby Museumplein. Rather than staring at paintings you'll never own, haggle for wares at **Albert Cuypmarkt** (see **Shopping**). Or, instead of contemplating what life would be like in the Dutch Golden Age, find out what it's like being a bottle of beer at the **Heineken Experience**.

Sarphatipark   PARK

In the 1860s, Amsterdam's chief architect was convinced that the center of the city would move south, and that this spot in De Pijp (then just marshlands and a windmill or two) would be the ideal place for Centraal Station. We all know how that one turned out (though we wonder what would have happened to the Red Light District if visitors couldn't stumble straight into it from the station). Not one to be deterred, the architect decided to build a park instead. Sarphatipark is fairly small, but its crisscrossing paths and central monument give it a genteel, 19th-century feel. It's rarely as crowded as Vondelpark, so you can have more grassy sunbathing space to yourself. The monument commemorates the park's namesake, the Jewish philanthropist and doctor Samuel Sarphati.

▶ 🚋 Tram #3 or 25 to 2e Van der Helstraat.

Heineken Experience   MUSEUM
Stadhouderskade 78
☎020 523 92 22; www.heinekenexperience.com

They can't call it a museum, because it isn't informative enough, and they can't call it a brewery, because beer hasn't been made here since 1988. So, welcome to the Heineken "Experience." Four floors of holograms, multimedia exhibits, and virtual-reality machines tell you everything you'll ever want to know about the green-bottled stuff. Highlights include a ride that replicates the experience of actually becoming a Heineken beer. (There's something very Zen-alcoholic about the whole "in order to enjoy the beer you must BE the beer" idea.) In the end, this is a big tourist trap where you pay €15 to watch an hour of Heineken commercials. On the other hand, there's something quintessentially Dutch about the whole "experience"—these are, after all, the people who invented capitalism.

▶ 🚋 Tram #16 or 24 to Stadhouderskade, or tram #4, 7, 10, or 25 to

Weterincircuit. From Weterincircuit, cross the canal and you'll see the building. Ⓢ €15. 🕐 Open daily 11am-7pm. Last entry 5:30pm.

JODENBUURT AND PLANTAGE

Some lesser-known but still worthwhile museums fill Jodenbuurt, historically the city's Jewish Quarter and now home to several sights focusing on Jewish culture and identity. Spacious Plantage, meanwhile, is home to the Botanical Gardens and Artis Zoo. The phenomenal Brouwerij 't IJ is in the north, by the water.

▧ Verzetsmuseum (Dutch Resistance Museum) MUSEUM

Plantage Kerklaan 61
☎020 620 25 35; www.verzetsmuseum.org

This museum chronicles the five years the Netherlands spent under Nazi occupation during WWII. The permanent exhibit centers on the question that people faced in this period, "What do we do?" In the early days of the occupation, many struggled to decided whether to adapt to their relatively unchanged life under Nazi rule or to resist. As time went on, the persecution of Jews, gypsies, and homosexuals intensified, and as repression grew, so did the resistance. The museum masterfully presents individuals' stories with interactive exhibits and an extensive collection of artifacts and video footage. The museum pays tribute to the ordinary Dutch citizens who risked (and often lost) their lives to publish illegal newspapers, hide Jews, or pass information to Allied troops. A smaller portion of the exhibit

Swimming with the Fishes

Move over, Atlantis. Rather than searching for the fabled underwater paradise, Dutch architects and city engineers have taken matters into their own hands. In 2018, construction will begin on an underwater city buried under canals. The underwater buildings would mostly be used for parking, shopping, and entertainment. The architects, Zwarts and Jansma, claim the project will be completely eco-friendly, and that the air filtration techniques will improve Amsterdam's above-ground air. Objectors to the project oppose the idea of living like moles under the earth—but we're pretty excited by the idea of living like mermen and mermaids, to be honest.

details the effects of the war on Dutch colonies in East Asia. Verzetsmuseum is well worth your time and money, even if you're not a history buff.

▶ ⁂ Tram #9 or 14 to Plantage Kerklaan. Across from Artis Zoo. ⓢ €7.50, ages 7-15 €4, under 7 and with Museumjaarkaart free. ⓘ Open M 11am-5pm, Tu-F 10am-5pm, Sa-Su 11am-5pm.

Tropenmuseum   MUSEUM

Linnaeusstraat 2
☎020 568 82 00; www.tropenmuseum.nl

In a palatial building that is part of the Koninklijk Instituut voor de Tropen (Dutch Royal Institute of the Tropics), this immense museum provides an anthropological look at the world's tropical regions from the distant past to today. A running theme throughout the exhibits is the complicated relationship between Europe and the tropics during the rise and fall of Western imperialism. An astounding collection of cultural artifacts like Thai bridal jewelry and African presidential folk cloths give a sense of life in these regions. An extensive portion of the first floor is devoted to the Dutch colonial experience in Indonesia (from the perspective of both the colonizers and colonized). There are also some cool interactive exhibits like drum kits to make early African music. That one's probably for the kids, but if you find yourself rocking out, we won't tell.

▶ ⁂ Tram #9, 10, or 14 to Alexanderplein. Cross the canal and walk left along Mauritskade. ⓢ €9, students €5, under 18 and with Museumjaarkaart free. ⓘ Open daily 10am-5pm.

Joods Historisch Museum
(Jewish Historical Museum)   MUSEUM

Nieuwe Amstelstraat 1
☎020 531 03 10; www.jhm.nl

Four 17th- and 18th-century Ashkenazi synagogues were incorporated to form this museum dedicated to the history and culture of Dutch Jews. One part of the museum highlights the religious life of the community using artifacts (including a number of beautifully decorated Torahs), explanations of Jewish traditions, and videos that recount personal anecdotes. Another exhibit explores the history of the community between 1600 and 1900, from the first settlements in this unusually tolerant city to later struggles to gain full civil and political liberties. The period surrounding WWII is also covered. The museum holds two temporary exhibition spaces that host art shows. The JHM Children's Museum introduces kids to Jewish life and culture through the reconstruction of a typical Jewish family, with friendly Max the Matzo as their guide.

▶ 🚋 Trams #9 or 14 or Ⓜ️Waterlooplein. Walk down Waterlooplein and turn right onto Wesperstraat. Nieuwe Amstelstraat is on the right. Ⓢ €9, students and seniors €6, ages 13-17 €4.50, under 13 and with Museumjaarkaart free. Special exhibits may cost extra. ⏰ Open daily 11am-5pm.

Brouwerij 't IJ   BREWERY
Funenkade 7
☎020 622 83 25; www.brouwerijhetij.nl

What could be more Dutch than drinking beer at the base of a windmill? Even better, the beer brewed and served here is much, much tastier than the more internationally famous Dutch brands. Once a bathhouse, this building was taken over as a squat in the 1980s. Today, its brewers craft 10 organic, unfiltered, and non-pasteurized beers. You can try a glass or three of their wares at the massive outdoor terrace of the on-site pub, or at cafes and bars throughout the city. The brewers are proud of their beers, which range from a golden triple beer to a pilsner; proud of their brewery, which you can scope out on a free tour; and even prouder of their huge collection of beer bottles, purportedly one of Europe's largest.

▶ 🚋 Tram #10 to Hoogte Kadijk or #14 to Pontanusstraat. Head toward the windmill. Ⓢ Beer €2. ⏰ Pub open daily 3-8pm. Free brewery tours F and Su 4pm.

Rembrandt House Museum   MUSEUM
Jodenbreestraat 4
☎020 520 04 00; www.rembrandthuis.nl

Flush with success at the height of his popularity, Rembrandt van Rijn bought this massively expensive house in 1639. Twenty years later, after a decline in sales and failure to pay his mortgage, he was forced to sell it along with many of his possessions. His misfortune turned out to be a great boon for historians—the inventory of Rembrandt's worldly goods gave curators the ability to reconstruct his house almost exactly as it was when he lived there. Now visitors can see where Rembrandt slept, entertained guests, made paintings, sold paintings, and got attacked by his mistress after a fight over alimony (that would be the kitchen). The most interesting rooms are on the top floor: Rembrandt's massive studio (with many of his original tools) and the room where he stored his *objets d'art*—armor, armadillos, and everything in between. Paintings by his talented contemporaries and students adorn the walls, and the museum holds a collection of hundreds of Rembrandt's etchings. Guides reenact his etching and printing techniques on the third floor every 45min.

▶ Tram #9 or 14 or ⓜWaterlooplein. Walk down Waterlooplein, around the stadium, then turn right and continue until you reach Jodenbreestraat. The museum is on the right. ⓢ €9, with ISIC card €6, ages 6-17 €2.50, under 6 and with Museumjaarkaart free. Open daily 10am-5pm.

Hortus Botanicus   GARDENS

Plantage Middenlaan 2A
☎020 638 16 70; www.dehortus.nl

One of the oldest botanical gardens in the world, Hortus Botanicus began in 1638 as a place for growing medicinal herbs (no, not that kind). Now it's grown to include over 4000 species of plant life. Thanks to the Dutch East India company, the gardens gathered exotic species from all around the world, and some of those original plants (such as the Eastern Cape giant cycad) are still around today. The "crown jewels" section is the place to go to catch a glimpse of extremely rare species such as the *Victoria amazonica,* a water lily that only opens at dusk. Nicely landscaped ponds and paths make this a pleasant place to wander for an afternoon, and the butterfly house might be the closest you'll get to some steamy summer weather in Amsterdam.

▶ Tram #9 or 14 to Mr. Visserplein. Walk down Plantage Middenlaan. The gardens are on the right. ⓢ €7.50, seniors and ages 5-14 €3.50. Tours €1. Open July-Aug M-F 9am-7pm, Sa-Su 10am-7pm; Sept-June M-F 9am-5pm, Sa-Su 10am-5pm. Tours Su 2pm.

Food

For some reason, when we think "Northern Europe," we don't think "awesome food." It's telling that in the vast world of Amsterdam restaurants, not too many of them actually serve Dutch cuisine. (Here's a quick run-down of what that looks like: pancakes, cheese, herring, and various meat-and-potato combinations.) Luckily, Amsterdam's large immigrant populations have brought Indonesian, Surinamese, Ethiopian, Algerian, Thai, and Chinese food to the banks of the canals. Finally, Amsterdam has this thing with sandwiches—they're everywhere, and they tend to be really, really good.

De Pijp, Jordaan, and the Nine Streets in Canal Ring West boast the highest concentration of quality eats, and De Pijp is the cheapest of the three. If you really want to conserve your cash, the supermarket chain Albert Heijn is a gift from the budget gods (find the nearest location at www.ah.nl). Keep in mind that most supermarkets close around 8pm. If you need groceries late at night (we can only guess why), try De Avondmarkt near Westerpark.

Budget Food

In a land where "coffeeshop" doesn't refer to Starbucks and red lights don't indicate stopping, the food scene is no different—it's weird. Most food in Amsterdam isn't traditional Dutch food, and if it is it's overpriced and borderline gross. Go to De Pijp, oh budget traveler, and indulge in more cheap, international fare than at a Simon Mall food court. If you don't feel like traveling across town, grab a cheap sandwich at one of the hundreds of places that specialize in them, or head to the local Albert Heijn supermarket and pick up some munchies.

OUDE ZIJD

Zeedijk is overrun with restaurants, but if you shop around to avoid touristy rip-offs, you can land a great meal.

'Skek   CAFE, GLOBAL $$
Zeedijk 4-8

☎020 427 05 51; www.skek.nl

A "cultural eetcafe" where students (with ID) get a 33% discount, 'Skek prepares healthy, hearty cuisine, with rotating options like a Japanese hamburger with wasabi mayonnaise, grilled vegetable lasagna, and braised eggplant. The interior is on a mission to be hip, with whimsical fantasy board games painted on the tables, student art on the walls, and occasional live music. Come for the free Wi-Fi and student discount, stay for the not-bad food—just don't accidentally order the hamburger made out of carrots.

▶ ✱ From Centraal Station, follow Prins Hendrikkade to Zeedijk. ⓢ Lunch dishes around €5-7. Dinner entrees around €13. ☼ Open M-Th noon-1am, F-Sa noon-3am, Su noon-1am.

Latei   CAFE $
Zeedijk 143

☎020 625 74 85; www.latei.net

Colorful and eccentric, Latei is filled with mismatched furniture and interesting knick-knacks—which just so happen to all be for sale. But save your money for the simple, filling, and tasty food: sandwiches are made with artisan bread and the cafe's own olive oil and topped with fresh cheese or veggies. (Note: Dutch "sandwiches" usually only include one slice of bread.) Indian cuisine makes a guest appearance at dinner Thursday to Saturday nights.

▶ 🚇 Ⓜ Nieuwmarkt. Zeedijk is along the northwestern corner of the square. Ⓢ Sandwiches €3-5. Desserts €3-4. 🕐 Open M-W 8am-6pm, Th-F 8am-10pm, Sa 9am-10pm, Su 11am-6pm.

Bird
THAI $$

Zeedijk 72-74

☎020 620 14 42; www.thai-bird.nl

Zeedijk may be considered Amsterdam's Chinatown, but the best Asian restaurant in town might be this Thai eatery. Across the street from the main restaurant is a simpler snack bar version, which sells many of the same dishes for a few euro less. The menu is full of all your favorite Thai classics, including some special dishes from the northeast. *Let's Go* really likes their green curry.

▶ 🚇 Ⓜ Nieuwmarkt. Ⓢ Entrees €8-14. Snack bar cash only. 🕐 Open daily 5-11pm. Snack bar open daily 2-10pm.

In de Waag
ITALIAN, DUTCH $$$

Nieuwmarkt 4

☎020 452 77 72; www.indewaag.nl

Located inside De Waag, Nieuwmarkt's distinctive 15th-century castle, this restaurant presents quite the dining experience—with prices to match. During the summer, sit on the large terrace and admire the architecture and bustle of the square. When it's cold out, the modernized medieval interior, lit by hundreds of candles, is just as enticing. The food is Mediterranean with a Dutch twist—lots of lamb, beef, and fish, with some vegetarian pastas and polentas.

▶ 🚇 Ⓜ Nieuwmarkt. Ⓢ Lunch entrees €7.50-14; dinner entrees €18-22. 🕐 Open daily 10am-1am.

RED LIGHT DISTRICT

Gluttony is one of the few sins you can't indulge in the Red Light District. There are plenty of snack shops selling plastic-looking pizzas and imitation falafel, but there are also some good, reasonably priced cafes. If you're looking for a quality meal, head next door to the Oude Zijd.

De Bakkerswinkel
CAFE $

Warmoesstraat 69

☎020 489 80 00; www.debakkerswinkel.nl

This place is as cute and homey as the surrounding streets are neon and sordid. In the large pastel dining room, you can enjoy quiche, breakfast, or homemade sourdough bread and cheese. High tea is also available, with different combinations of scones, sweets, and sandwiches. Dessert here is a special treat, befitting the general decadence of the neighborhood.

▶ ♯ From Centraal Station, walk down Damrak, turn left onto Oudebrugsteeg, and then right onto Warmoesstraat. ⓢ Sandwiches €4. Slice of quiche €5. Breakfast menus €6-12. High teas €14-40. ⏲ Open Tu-F 8am-6pm, Sa 8am-5pm, Su 10am-5pm.

Si Chaun Kitchen   CHINESE $
Warmoesstraat 17
☎020 420 78 33

Chinese is probably the best deal for a substantial meal in the Red Light District, and Si Chaun is marginally cozier, cheaper, and tastier than many of its competitors. This place offers standard favorites like fried rice and noodle dishes alongside house specialties and plenty of vegetarian options.

▶ ♯ From Centraal Station, walk down Damrak, turn left onto Oudebrugsteeg, and left onto Warmoesstraat. ⓢ Most entrees €7-12. ⏲ Open daily 3-11:30pm.

NIEUWE ZIJD

Eating in the Nieuwe Zijd is less than ideal: the area is packed with overpriced, low-quality tourist traps. Try the southern half of **Spuistraat** or head to one of the shopping-center cafeterias nearby for a quick lunch. Otherwise, save your money and head to the Canal Ring West instead.

◪ Cafe Schuim   CAFE $
Spuistraat 189
☎020 638 93 57

This artsy cafe offers a nice break from the neighborhood's usual big chains, with old movie posters adorning the walls and massive, padded leather chairs. Try the smoked chicken and avocado club for lunch, or the creative pasta or steak at dinner. Cafe Schuim is popular at night, too, when young professionals and hipsters crowd the bar and picnic tables outside. Live music and DJs perform a few times per month.

▶ ♯ Tram #1, 2, 5, or 14 to Dam/Paleisstraat. Walk down Paleisstraat toward Singel and make a left onto Spuistraat. ⓢ Sandwiches €4-7. Pasta €9.50-13. Beer from €2.20. ⏲ Open M-Th noon-1am, F-Sa noon-3am, Su 1pm-1am.

La Place   CAFETERIA $
Kalverstraat 203
☎020 622 01 71; www.laplace.nl

In most parts of Amsterdam, cute cafes tend to be the best informal dining choice. In the Nieuwe Zijd, many of those cafes will charge €10 for a sandwich, so embrace the rampant commercialism and head to this immense multi-level cafeteria inside the giant **Vroom and Dreesmann** department store. You'll be rewarded with a vast, affordable buffet of pizza, pasta, salad, sandwiches, meats, and pastries. Grab a tray and help yourself, then head to one of several seating areas, including an outdoor terrace. Of the many cafeterias and food courts nearby, this is the biggest and the grandest.

▶ Tram #4, 9, 14, 16, 24, or 25 to Muntplein. Note the giant V and D store, and enter through the Kalverstraat door. The entrance to the cafeteria is on the left. $ Sandwiches €3-5. Pizzas €7. Entrees typically €3-8. Open M 11am-8pm, Tu-W 10am-8pm, Th 10am-9pm, F-Sa 10am-8pm, Su noon-8pm.

Ristorante Caprese   ITALIAN $$
Spuistraat 259-261
☎020 620 00 59

The service here is leisurely at best, but that just makes it feel more authentically Italian. With the massive wall mural of the Bay of Naples, you might even be convinced that you're a few countries to the south. Ristorante Caprese serves traditional Italian food done well, from the excellent tomato sauce to the organically raised meat.

▶ Tram #1, 2, or 5 to Spui/Nieuwezijds Voorburgwal. Cross over to Spuistraat and turn right. $ Pasta €9-14. Meat entrees €18-22. House wine from €4. Open daily noon-11pm.

Sie Joe   INDONESIAN $
Gravenstraat 24
☎020 624 18 30; www.siejoe.com

This unassuming Indonesian spot in the shadow of the Nieuwe Kerk is one of the best cheap options for a sit-down meal in the area. The limited menu contains a half-dozen rice dishes, some soups, and meat satays. For vegetarians, the *gado gado* (mixed vegetables and tofu in peanut sauce) is a good option.

▶ From Dam Sq., walk up Nieuwezijds Voorburgwal and turn left onto Gravenstraat. Sie Joe is directly behind the church. $ Entrees €6.75-9.25. Open M-W noon-7pm, Th noon-8pm, F-Sa noon-7pm.

SCHEEPVAARTBUURT

Haarlemmerstraat and **Haarlemmerdijk** are lined with restaurants, from cheap sandwich joints to upscale bistros. You'll have no problem finding somewhere to eat, but don't disregard the quality options off the main streets.

Harlem: Drinks and Soul Food　　　　AMERICAN $$
Haarlemmerstraat 77
☎020 330 14 98

No, they didn't leave out a vowel: this place is the Dutch outpost of good ol' American soul food (or, at least, as close to it as you'll get in the Netherlands). At Harlem, you can indulge your culinary homesickness without the shame of being seen in a Burger King. Fill up on a variety of club sandwiches, soups, and salads at lunch or sup on dishes like fried chicken at dinner. As the night wears on, patrons stick around to imbibe and listen to the grooving soul and funk on the stereo, making Harlem one of Scheepvaartbuurt's livelier places come nightfall.

▶ ✝ From Centraal Station, turn right, cross the Singel, and walk down Haarlemmerstraat a few blocks. Harlem is on the corner with Herenmarkt. ⓢ Sandwiches €5-8. Entrees €12-18. ⓓ Open M-Th 10am-1am, F-Sa 10am-3am, Su 10am-1am. Kitchen closes at 10pm.

Open Cafe-Restaurant　　　　MEDITERRANEAN $$
Westerdoksplein 20
☎020 620 10 10; www.open.nl

This restaurant inhabits one of the coolest locations in Amsterdam—a renovated segment of a train bridge perched high above the water, between Westerdok and the IJ. You can sit in the glossy interior (lined with windows and green leather booths), on a walkway terrace, or on the sidewalk right by the water. The Mediterranean-style food is elegant, and includes dishes like lamb ravioli, stewed oxtail, and sea-bass salad. Most dishes come in both half and full portions.

▶ ✝ From Haarlemmerstraat, walk from Korte Prinsengracht through the tunnel under the train tracks and then cross the bridge. Open is on the right. ⓢ Sandwiches and salads €7-14. Half-entrees €7-14; full €14-22. ⓓ Open daily 10am-10:30pm.

Le Sud
VEGETARIAN, MEDITERRANEAN $

Haarlemmerdijk 118

☎064 019 04 49; www.lesud.nl

This counter near Haarlemmerplein sells a variety of salads and vegetarian sandwiches filled with things like hummus, grilled eggplant, and falafel. There's also a tremendous array of deli items, including olives, cheeses, dolmades (stuffed grape leaves), tapenades, and more hummus. Food is primarily for takeout.

▶ 🚊 Tram #3 to Haarlemmerplein. Cross Haarlemmerplein to reach Haarlemmerdijk, then continue walking east. Ⓢ Sandwiches €3. Salads €1.25-2.50 per 100g. 🕙 Open M-Sa 10am-6pm.

CANAL RING WEST

This is one of the best places for high-quality eats in Amsterdam. The Nine Streets area is packed with hip and delicious cafes.

🛡 'T Kuyltje
SANDWICHES $

Gasthuismolensteeg 9

☎020 620 10 45; www.kuyltje.nl

This no-frills takeout spot makes tremendous, filling Belgian *broodjes* (sandwich rolls). The proprietor used to be a butcher, a fact which is immediately evident from the fresh and flavorful meats (roast beef, pastrami, speck, etc.) hanging from the ceiling.

▶ 🚊 Tram #1, 2, 5, 13, 14, or 17 to Dam/Radhuisstraat. Continue down Radhuisstraat and make a left at the Singel. Ⓢ Sandwiches €3-4. 🕙 Open M-F 7am-4pm.

🛡 Tasca Bellota
SPANISH $$

Herenstraat 22

☎020 420 29 46; www.tascabellota.com

Spanish restaurants are hugely popular in Amsterdam, but few match the quality and value of this tapas-and-wine bar. The menu features delicious dishes like spicy lamb meatballs, peppers stuffed with lentils and Manchego cheese, and dates with bacon. The interior is intimate, and its murals have a bullfighter fetish that would put Hemingway to shame. Strongly recommended by locals, Tasca Bellota also hosts live music some nights.

▶ 🚊 Tram #1, 2, 5, 13, or 17 to Nieuwezijds Kolk. Cross Spuistraat and the Singel and continue on Herenstraat. Ⓢ Small dishes €5-10. 🕙 Open Tu-Su 6-10pm.

Dutch Nom Nom

Ordering a meal at a Dutch restaurant is no easy affair. The names of many Dutch dishes contain more letters than the dishes do calories. Educate yourself on the meanings of these common Dutch delicacies in order to ensure you get a sweet deal.

- **jan-in-de-zal.** This "john in the bag" is no evil twin to SNL's "dick in a box." Also known as "plum duff," this dessert consists of a ball of dough stuffed with candied lemon peels and slices of roasted almonds, all cooked in a pot of boiling water. Before you ask, changing the name to "ball in a pot" probably wouldn't help with the sexual connotations.

- **Boerenjongens.** Is this just us, or does this all sound like sex stuff? Boerenjongens are just brandied raisins, and frequently appear at the bottom of a cup of eggnog.

- **Kapucijners.** This bean is not for cappuccino-lovers. Rather than deriving its name from any coffee drink, the pea-like Kapucijners gets its name from its color, which is reminiscent of the habits of Capuchin monks.

- **Kip met slagroomsaus.** This isn't some Martian version of When Harry Met Sally. This dish, which translates to "chicken with whipped cream sauce," involves a light, airy cream usually made with onions or mushrooms.

De Kaaskamer   CHEESE $$
Runstraat 7
☎020 623 34 83; www.kaaskamer.nl

Wallace and Gromit's dream come true, this store is packed floor-to-ceiling with hundreds of types of cheese. Hard cheese, soft cheese, French cheese, Dutch cheese, red cheese, blue cheese—if you can make it out of milk, they have it. Because man cannot live on cheese alone (though one ill-fated *Let's Go* researcher tried it a few years back), the shop also sells wine, bread, olives, and other cheese-complementing snacks. This is Holland: you want to go to a cheese shop. Go to this one.

▶ 🚋 Tram #13, 14, or 17 to Westermarkt. Walk down Prinsengracht and Runstraat will be on the left. ⓢ Most cheeses €2-5 per 100g, €7-9 per 500g. Cash only. 🕐 Open M noon-6pm, Tu-F 9am-6pm, Sa 9am-5pm, Su noon-5pm.

The Pancake Bakery   DUTCH $$
Prinsengracht 191
☎020 625 13 33; www.pancake.nl

Many swear that this canal-side restaurant serves the best pancakes in Amsterdam. The menu has a dizzying list of sweet and savory options, from the standard ham and cheese to international concoctions like the Indonesian (with chicken, peanut sauce, and sprouts). Enjoy these flaky, gooey wonders in the wooden interior or at a table by the water. The bakery also serves beer and cherry jenever—because the only thing better than fat and happy is fat, happy, and drunk.

▶ 🚋 Tram #13, 14, or 17 to Westermarkt. Make a right up Prinsengracht. Ⓢ Pancakes €7-14. 🕓 Open daily noon-9:30pm.

Vennington   CAFE $
Prinsenstraat 2
☎020 625 93 98

Vennington is an inexpensive, diner-esque restaurant that serves breakfast and lunch. There's nothing particularly gourmet going on here; it's just a place to get full and have a nice greasy meal for as few euro as possible. They have an extensive selection of sandwiches breakfast items, coffee, and shakes.

▶ 🚋 From the Westerkerk, walk up Prinsengracht and make a right. Ⓢ Sandwiches €2.50-7. Coffee from €1.50. Shakes €3-4. 🕓 Open daily 8am-5:30pm.

CENTRAL CANAL RING

You'll eat well in the Central Canal Ring, where restaurants are affordable, tourist crowds are low, and you're never too far from Amsterdam's major sights. Try window-food-shopping down **Utrechtsestraat,** which is full of tasty ethnic eateries, Dutch cheese shops, and bakery fronts piled high with pastries—it's a little like food porn's answer to the Red Light District.

🔖 Zuivere Koffie   CAFE $
Utrechtsestraat 39
☎020 624 99 99

There's an expression in Dutch, *"dat is geen zuivere koffie,"* which translates to, "that's no pure coffee," but really means something like, "that's totally suspicious." This cozy store is the opposite, offering good coffee and delicious homemade croissants, desserts, and sandwiches. The apple pie is a thing of beauty. Feel comfortably European while enjoying it all in the gorgeous garden seating area.

▶ 🚋 Tram #4, 16, 24, or 25 to Keizersgracht. Walk east on Keizersgracht and make a left onto Utrechtsestraat. ⑤ Sandwiches €5. Apple pie €3.50. Drinks €2-4. ⏰ Open M-F 8am-5pm, Sa 9am-5pm.

🏛 Golden Temple   VEGETARIAN $$
Utrechtsestraat 126
☎020 626 85 60; www.restaurantgoldentemple.com

Golden Temple offers a new-age soundtrack, yoga classes, and a tiny roof terrace with sofas and Indian artwork. But none of that will matter once you taste the food. The dinner menu features vegetarian cuisine, from salads to Italian pizzas to Mediterranean *mezze*. The food is a bit on the pricey side, but Golden Temple takes its ingredients seriously, and the meals are delicious and filling.

▶ 🚋 Tram #4, 7, 10, or 25 to Fredericksplein. Walk diagonally through the square and up Utrechtsestraat. *i* Free Wi-Fi. ⑤ Entrees €8-17. ⏰ Open daily 5-9:30pm.

B and B Lunchroom   CAFE, SANDWICHES $
Leidsestraat 44
☎020 638 15 42

It's hard to walk by this storefront window heaped high with pastries and muffins and not drool with desire. Unlike so many bakeries in town, most people can actually afford to step inside this one and indulge. You can probably even afford a real meal too. Filling sandwiches feature healthy and tasty combinations like roast beef and "citron mayonnaise," or gorgonzola and asparagus. Soups and salads complete the extensive menu printed on blackboards across the store. In the afternoon, you may have to take your food to go, as the store gets busy with locals on lunch break.

▶ 🚋 Tram #1, 2, or 5 to Keizersgracht. The cafe is on the southwestern corner. ⑤ Sandwiches €3.50-6. Salads €6.50-7.50. ⏰ Open daily 10am-6pm.

LEIDSEPLEIN

Korte and Lange Leidsedwarsstraat are stuffed with restaurants of every kind. Most post menus and prices (and sometimes enthusiastic, soliciting hostesses) outside, making it a little easier to shop around and avoid rip-offs. For the best values, look for restaurants that have special set menus or daily deals, or just grab a sandwich and snack from a grocery store. At night, places like **Maoz** and **Wok to Walk** (both on Leidsestraat, toward Prinsengracht) stay open late and are surprisingly tasty and affordable.

Bojo
INDONESIAN $$

Lange Leidsedwarsstraat 49

☎020 643 44 43

Come here for great deals on delectable Indonesian cuisine. Bojo offers several special combo deals, including your choice of meat, noodle or rice dish, and a satay skewer (€10). The portions are ample, and the staff knows it—there's a note on the menu encouraging visitors to ask for a doggy bag. The bamboo walls and low-hanging lanterns will make you think you're oceans away from chilly Amsterdam.

▶ 🚋 Tram #1, 2, 5, 7, or 10 to Leidseplein. Walk down Leidseplein, turn left onto Leidsekruisstraat, and then left onto Lange Leidsekruisstraat. Ⓢ Entrees €8-14. 🕐 Open M-F 4-9pm, Sa-Su noon-9pm.

De Zotte
BELGIAN $$

Raamstraat 29

☎020 626 86 94; www.dezotte.nl

De Zotte is unusual among the infinite alcohol-focused establishments around the Leidseplein thanks to its attention to quality, not just quantity. It offers a wide selection of beers and a menu full of hearty Belgian food to go with them. Choose from steak, sausages, and pâté or cheese served with wonderful country bread. Less artery-clogging options like quiche are also available.

▶ 🚋 Tram #7 or 10 to Raamplein. Raamstraat is 1 block away from the Leidsegracht. Or tram #1, 2, or 5 to Leidseplein. Walk down Marnixstraat and Raamstraat is on the right after the canal. Ⓢ Appetizers (some are filling enough to be a meal) from €3. Entrees €10-17. 🕐 Open M-Th 4pm-1am, Sa-Su 4pm-3am. Kitchen open daily 6-9:30pm.

The Pantry
DUTCH $$

Leidsekruisstraat 21

☎020 620 09 22; www.thepantry.nl

Designed to feel like an old Dutch living room, with traditional paintings and cozy wooden tables, The Pantry fills up with locals, as well as tourists brave enough to try some authentic Dutch dishes, like salted herring and *boerenkoolstamppot* (mashed potatoes mixed with kale, served with a smoked sausage or meatball).

► 🚊 Tram #1, 2, 5, 7, or 10 to Leidseplein. Make a right onto Korte Leidsedwarsstraat and Leidsekruisstraat is on the left. ⓢ Entrees €12-17. 🕑 Open daily noon-9pm.

J. J. Ooijevaar DELI $
Lange Leidsedwarsstraat 47
☎020 623 55 03

This is the place for the cheapest sandwiches on the Leidseplein—perhaps in all of Amsterdam. Rolls start at €1.30, and all kinds of fillings (cheeses, meats, vegetables, etc.) are available to stuff inside them. They also sell dirt-cheap grocery and convenience items.

► 🚊 Tram #1, 2, 5, 7, or 10 to Leidseplein. Walk down Leidseplein, take a left onto Leidsekruisstraat, and another left onto Lange Leidsekruisstraat. ⓢ Sandwiches €1.30-3.50. 6-pack of beer €6. 🕑 Open M-F 8:30am-6pm.

REMBRANDTPLEIN

Rembrandtplein, like the Leidseplein, is packed with enormous international restaurants and oversized cafes, but here there are fewer small, affordable eateries scattered into the mix. Below are the noteworthy exceptions.

🍴 Van Dobben SANDWICHES $
Korte Reguliersdwarsstraat 5-9
☎020 624 42 00; www.eetsalonvandobben.nl

An old-school deli and cafeteria that is everything most restaurants in Rembrandtplein are not: cheap, fast, and simple. The black and white ceramic tiling and chrome accents are a good match for the food's simplicity. Choose from a long list of sandwiches or a more limited selection of soups, salads, and omelettes. We're not sure how this place stays in business, seeing as everywhere else nearby seems to charge five times as much, but keep it in mind when looking for a satisfying meal for under €10 in this neighborhood.

► 🚊 Tram #9 or 14 to Rembrandtplein. The easiest way to find the small street is to get onto Reguliersdwarsstraat heading away from Rembrandtplein, and then look for where the street veers off on the right. *i* Free Wi-Fi. ⓢ Sandwiches €2.50-5. 🕑 Open M-W 10am-9pm, Th 10am-1am, F-Sa 10am-2am, Su 11:30am-8pm.

🍴 Ristorante Pizzeria Firenze   ITALIAN $

Halvemaansteeg 9-11

☎020 627 33 60; www.pizzeria-firenze.nl

The plentitude of pizzas and murals of Italian scenery on the walls will make you feel like you're actually in *Italia*. By no means is it the world's best pizza, but when you can get a huge pie for only €5-7, no one's complaining. With dozens of choices for both pizza and pasta, as well as some meat and fish dishes, Pizzeria Firenze is definitely one of the best values for a restaurant meal around Rembrandtplein.

▶ 🚋 Tram #9 or 14 to Rembrandtplein. Halvemaansteeg is the street to the left of the line of buildings with the giant TV screen. ⓢ Pizza and pasta €5-11. House wine €2.50 per glass. 🕐 Open daily 1-11pm.

Rose's Cantina   MEXICAN $$

Reguliersdwarsstraat 40

☎020 625 97 97; www.rosescantina.com

A bright interior with salsa music and an outdoor patio make this a livelier option among the similarly overpriced restaurants around Rembrandtplein. They have a good selection of appetizers and standard Mexican entrees. The large bar serves up a long list of summery cocktails.

▶ 🚋 Tram #9 or 14 to Rembrandtplein or tram #1, 2, or 5 to Koningsplein. ⓢ Appetizers €5.50-7.50. Entrees €14-21. Mixed drinks €7-9.50. 🕐 Open M-Th 5-10:30pm, F-Sa 5pm-2am, Su 5-10:30pm. Kitchen closes F-Sa at 11pm.

JORDAAN

The Jordaan has very few truly budget food options, but few overpriced ones either. Establishments here are frequented more by loyal regulars than by tourists.

🍴 Rainarai   ALGERIAN $$

Prinsengracht 252

☎020 624 97 91; www.rainarai.nl

The Algerian dishes at this small food counter change daily, and the staff will explain the day's offerings to you. A standard plate (get the medium) comes with generous servings of rice or couscous, a meat dish, and a vegetable dish, including items like spicy lamb meatballs, grilled asparagus, stuffed artichokes, and curry. Take-out is available, and serious fans can take home the store's cookbook or some Algerian spices from the mini grocery.

▶ 🚋 Tram #13, 14, or 17 to Westermarkt. Cross Prinsengracht and turn left. Ⓢ Medium entree plate €13.50. ⏰ Open Tu-Su noon-10pm.

De Vliegende Schotel   VEGETARIAN $$

Nieuwe Leliestraat 162-168

☎020 625 20 41; www.vliegendeschotel.com

With hearty dishes and generous portions, De Vliegende Schotel, "The Flying Saucer," is the perfect place to grab dinner after exploring 🔆**Electric Ladyland.** The organic and vegan-friendly menu changes seasonally, but often includes dishes like Ayurvedic curry, seitan goulash, or lasagna. You may have to wait for your food—after all, it's prepared from scratch in the open kitchen by the eccentric old proprietor.

▶ 🚋 Tram #10 to Bloemgracht. Cross Lijnbaansgracht, turn left, and then right onto Nieuwe Leliestraat. Ⓢ Entrees €11-13. ⏰ Open daily 4-11:30pm. Kitchen closes at 10:45pm.

Winkel   CAFE $$

Noordermarkt 43

☎020 623 02 23; www.winkel43.nl

It's all about the famous apple pie here, renowned across the city and served with a heap of fluffy whipped cream. Don't be surprised if every person inside has a plate of it. Enjoy your pie and the view from the outdoor patio, or step into the quaint interior and chat with locals. Not up for dessert? Winkel serves up sandwiches, soups, and stews, and occasionally hosts live music and dancing. Besides the pie, the food isn't too memorable, but it has a nice location and isn't too expensive.

▶ 🚋 Tram #3 or 10 to Marnixplein. Cross Lijnbaangracht, walk up Westerstraat, and make a left onto Noordermarkt Sq. Ⓢ Entrees €6-15. ⏰ Open M 7am-1am, Tu-Th 8am-1am, F 8am-3am, Sa 7am-3am, Su 10am-1am.

Toscanini   ITALIAN $$$$

Lindengracht 75

☎020 623 28 13; www.diningcity.nl/toscanini

Quite a few locals swear backward and forward that this is the best Italian food in Amsterdam. The menu is strongly authentic: instead of pizza, you'll find homemade pastas like ravioli with lemon and saffron, or *secondi* like pan-fried pork with *vin santo*. The bright, sky-lit interior lacks the gimmickry of faux-Italian trattorias the world over. Since it's been around

for over 20 years, Toscanini is no longer a secret, so reservations are almost always required.
- 🚋 Tram #3 to Nieuwe Willemstraat. Cross Lijnbaansgracht to Willemstraat, turn right onto Palmdwarsstraat, and then left onto Lindengracht. Ⓢ Appetizers €11-15. *Primi* €8-15. S*econdi* €18-23. ⌚ Open M-Sa 6-10:30pm.

WESTERPARK AND OUD-WEST

Some of the best-quality food can be found in these residential neighborhoods, where you're likely to be the only foreigner at the table.

🍴 Tomatillo   MEXICAN $
Overtoom 261
☎020 683 30 86; www.tomatillo.nl

Fresh ingredients, generous portions, and prices perfect for the budget-conscious set Tomatillo apart from the rest of the ethnic fast-food eateries along Overtoom. Familiar Tex-Mex is prepared in an open-air kitchen, visible from the clean, crisp dining area. The food steers clear of the greasy, over-cheesiness of many gringo attempts at Mexican cuisine. The tacos are an especially good deal, consisting of two small tortillas and a heap of fillings that add up to a satisfying lunch. You may feel strange listening to "Georgia on Your Mind" while you eat, but the English menu makes this a good option in a neighborhood that's not always foreigner-friendly.

- 🚋 Tram #1 to J. P. Heijestraat. Tomatillo is between Jan Pieter Heijestraat and G. Brandstraat, a block north of Vondelpark. Ⓢ Tacos €2.75-3.50. Burritos and tostadas €7.50-9.50. Desserts €2-4. ⌚ Open Tu-Su noon-9pm.

🍴 Bella Storia   ITALIAN $$
Bentinckstraat 28
☎020 488 05 99; www.bellastoria.info

For people who miss their Italian granny's home cooking (or missed out on having an Italian granny entirely), this is the place to be. It's truly a family affair, run by a mother and her sons who chatter in Italian as they roll out dough. Since the restaurant sits in the middle of an extremely residential area, expect to have the place to yourself during a weekday lunch and to be surrounded by locals at dinner. The daily specials aren't always listed on the menu, so check the blackboard or ask the waitress when you come in. We promise you won't be disappointed.

- 🚋 Tram #10 to Van Limburg Stirumplein. Facing Limburg Stirumstraat, Bentinckstraat is on your right. Ⓢ Pasta €10-17. ⌚ Open daily 10am-10pm.

Breakfast Sprinkles

Though the limited toast and jam in your hostel may suggest otherwise, the Dutch are pretty big on breakfast. They also have a fondness for desserts (name a culture that doesn't). In the 1930s, supposedly in response to a very persistent five-year-old boy who kept writing letters asking for a chocolate breakfast item, a Dutch company invented a great way to combine the two: *hagelslag*.

This confection is essentially chocolate sprinkles, but it provides a socially acceptable way to eat a ton of chocolate first thing in the morning: just sprinkle a thick layer of *hagelslag* on a piece of buttered toast. In addition to the original chocolate flavor, vanilla and fruit combinations exist. Still, legally, *hagelslag* must be over 35% cacao to be called *chocolat hagelslag*. Otherwise, the appropriate term is "cacao fantasy *hagelslag*"— which sounds like something unicorns eat.

De Avondmarkt   GROCERY STORE $
De Wittenkade 94-96
☎020 686 49 19; www.deavondmarkt.nl

One of the most frustrating things about the Netherlands can be the lack of 24hr. stores, but "The Evening Market" helps fill the bellies of night owls (at least until midnight). De Avondmarkt sells standard but high-quality groceries, wine, beer, cheeses, and prepared foods like lasagna. De Avondmarkt will also appeal to travelers looking for organic, cage-free, and vegan foods at affordable prices.

▶ ✈ Tram #10 to De Wittenkade. On the mainland side of De Wittenkade, at the corner of Van Limburg Stirumstraat. ⏰ Open M-F 4pm-midnight, Sa 3pm-midnight, Su 2pm-midnight.

Peperwortel   DELI $$
Overtoom 140
☎020 685 10 53; www.peperwortel.nl

The type of bountiful gourmet market you'd expect to find in Italy or France, Peperwortel offers prepared foods such as quiche, pasta, hummus, soup, and more exotic dishes like Indonesian beef. Order an entree as a meal, and it comes with a starch and vegetable. A wide variety of vegetarian options and a good wine selection round out the menu. Limited seating is available outside, but the grass of Vondelpark a few blocks away makes for an even better table.

▶ 🚋 Tram #1 to 1e Con. Huygensstraat. Peperwortel is on the corner of Overtoom and 2e Con. Huygensstraat. ⓢ Entrees €9-14. Desserts €3. Wines from €7. ⏰ Open M-F 4-9pm, Sa-Su 3-9pm.

Cafe Nassau
CAFE, ITALIAN $$

De Wittenkade 105A

☎020 684 35 62; www.cafenassau.com

Get your cute European cafe fix at this local favorite. Ingredients are fresh, and the helpful staff will guide you though the all-Dutch menu. Quaint outdoor patio furniture and picnic tables allow you to dine canal-side, and if you're lucky you can even land the table for two with the covered porch swing, perfect for taking that hostel romance to a classier level. Try the *broodje* (with spicy Italian sausage, grilled eggplant, parmesan, and arugula), sip on a Dutch coffee, or order a drink from the cafe's full bar.

▶ 🚋 Tram #10 to De Wittenkade. At the corner of De Wittenkade and 2e Nassaustraat. ⓢ Sandwiches from €5. Entrees €10-20. ⏰ Open M-Th 11:30am-midnight, F-Sa 11:30am-1am, Su 11:30am-midnight.

MUSEUMPLEIN AND VONDELPARK

Museumplein seems to be the one area of Amsterdam that consistently attracts real grown-ups, so food here tends to be a bit pricey. A long day of museum-hopping can be strenuous though, and the **Albert Heijn** supermarket right behind the van Gogh museum is the place to refuel on the cheap.

🏆 Cafe Vertigo
CAFE, MEDITERRANEAN $$

Vondelpark 3

☎020 612 30 21; www.vertigo.nl

Cafe Vertigo is housed in a remarkable, ornate building with a seemingly endless patio that makes it look like it should be more expensive than it is. On a summer day, there's no better place to enjoy a sandwich and a drink—except, perhaps, for the grass of Vondelpark itself. Sandwiches (like goat cheese with red onion compote) and soups (try the chickpea with lamb) make a great lunch. There's a full bar as well, so you can enjoy the atmosphere with just a drink too.

▶ 🚋 Tram #1, 3, or 12 to 1e Con. Huygensstraat/Overtoom. Walk down 1e Con. Huygensstraat, make a right onto Vondelstraat, enter the park about 1 block down, and the cafe is on the left. ⓢ Soups and sandwiches €3.50-6.75. Entrees €12-20. ⏰ Open daily 10am-1am.

🍴 Pasta Tricolore   ITALIAN $
P.C. Hooftstraat 52

☎020 664 83 14; www.pastatricolore.nl

If you want something a bit snazzier than Albert Heijn, Pasta Tricolore's front counter brims with a mouth-watering selection of salads, antipasti, lasagna, and desserts. You can also head to the back of the shop to order from a long list of Italian sandwiches (with filling combinations of salami, cheeses, and grilled vegetables). Limited seating is available, but it's nicest to take your meal to go and enjoy it in Vondelpark or Museumplein.

▶ 🚊 Tram #2 or 5 to Hobbemastraat. Walk down Hobbemastraat away from the Rijksmuseum and make a left onto P.C. Hooftstraat. 💲 Sandwiches and salads from €4. 🕐 Open M-Sa 9am-7pm, Su noon-7pm.

DE PIJP

If you could somehow eat every meal in De Pijp, you would be a happy camper. In a radius of just a few blocks, you'll find a tremendous variety of cuisine dished up at significantly lower prices than in most other parts of the city. **Albert Cuypstraat** and **Ferdinand Bolstraat** are good places to start, but there are plenty of great options on side streets as well. Many of the bars in De Pijp also whip up surprisingly good food.

🍴 Cafe De Pijp   MEDITERRANEAN $
Ferdinand Bolstraat 17-19

☎020 670 41 61; www.goodfoodgroup.nl

A catch-all local hotspot, Cafe De Pijp is usually swarmed with 20-somethings lingering over drinks, dinner, or more drinks. The menu has tapas-style offerings, like *merguez* (sausage) with Turkish bread and aioli, but also more substantial dishes, dishes like eggplant parmesan. On weekend nights, DJs spin dance tunes to help you work off your meal.

▶ 🚊 Tram #16 or 24 to Stadhouderskade. Walk 2 blocks down Ferdinand Bolstraat. Cafe De Pijp is on the left. 💲 Entrees €5.50-8. 🕐 Open M-Th 3:30pm-1am, F 3:30pm-3am, Sa noon-2am, Su noon-1am.

🍴 Het Ijspaleis   ICE CREAM $
1e Sweelinckstraat 20

☎061 204 16 17

This is a gleaming white "Ice Palace" that looks awfully tempting on a hot day, especially after trawling through the crowds of Albert Cuypmarkt. They serve up about a dozen fresh, homemade flavors in cups or cones, along with coffee and tea if you get too chilly. Keeping to the neighborhood's hipster ambience, they offer exotic flavors like rooibos, but don't miss the stroopwafel ice cream.

▶ 🚋 Tram #16 or 24 to Albert Cuypmarkt. Walk through the market and turn right. ⓢ Scoops from €1.10. ⓘ Open daily 11am-8pm.

🐾 Bazar   MIDDLE EASTERN $$

Albert Cuypstraat 182

☎020 675 05 44; www.bazaramsterdam.com

When the crush of Albert Cuypmarkt starts to feel a little overwhelming, pop into this church-cum-restaurant for inexpensive and tasty Middle Eastern. You can be basic with falafel or less basic with creative dinner specials like saffron veggie kebab. The vaulted ceilings are now decorated with Arabic Coca-Cola signs and old Dutch advertisements. Seating is available on the ground floor and in the old balconies above.

▶ 🚋 Tram #16 or 24 to Albert Cuypstraat. Walk through the market about 3 blocks. ⓢ Sandwiches and lunch entrees €4-10. Dinner entrees €12-16. ⓘ Open M-Th 11am-midnight, F 11am-1am, Sa 9am-1am, Su 9am-midnight.

Warung Spang Makandra   INDONESIAN $

Gerard Doustraat 39

☎020 670 50 81; www.spangmakandra.nl

Imperialism had more than a few downsides, but it was good at fostering new culinary combinations, like the Indonesian-Surinamese cuisine at this neighborhood favorite. Enjoy noodle and rice dishes, satays, and *rotis*—pancakes with meat and vegetable fillings—for incredibly low prices.

▶ 🚋 Tram #16 or 24 to Albert Cuypstraat. Walk 1 block north on Ferdinand Bolstraat and take the 1st left. The restaurant is on the left. ⓢ Entrees €5.50-9. ⓘ Open M-Sa 11am-10pm, Su 1-10pm.

De Soepwinkel   SOUP $

1e Sweelinckstraat 19F

☎020 673 22 83; www.soepwinkel.nl

Modern minimalism meets home cooking at this soup shop. Enjoy one of De Soepwinkel's six marvelous rotating soups (at least one is always vegetarian) inside the airy store or on the outside patio. They prepare quiches, tarts, and sandwiches as well.

▶ 🚋 Tram #3, 4, or 25 to Ceinturbaan/Van Woutstraat. Walk toward the park, turn right onto Sarphatipark, continue for 1½ blocks, and turn left onto 1e Sweelinckstraat. Alternatively, take tram #16 or 24 to Albert Cuypstraat. Walk a few blocks through the market and turn right onto 1e Sweelinckstraat. ⓢ Soups from €4. Menu with soup, a slice of quiche, and a drink €8.50. ☼ Open M-F 11am-8pm, Sa 11am-6pm.

Burgermeester

BURGERS $

Albert Cuypstraat 48

☎020 670 93 39; www.burgermeester.eu

Thankfully, the burgers here are better than the store's punny name (*burgemeester* is "mayor" in Dutch). This is something of a designer-burger bar—you can get a patty made from fancy beef, lamb, salmon, falafel, or Manchego cheese and hazelnuts, then top it with Chinese kale, truffle oil, or buffalo mozzarella. Burgers can be ordered normal-sized or miniature. They sell salads, too, but who goes to a burger joint for a salad?

▶ ⓕ Tram #16 or 24 to Albert Cuypstraat. Walk down the street away from the market. ⓢ Burgers €6.50-8.50. Toppings €0.50-1. ☼ Open daily noon-11pm.

Wild Moa Pies

PIES $

Van Ostadestraat 147

☎064 291 40 50; www.pies.nu

We didn't know that New Zealand had much national cuisine, but apparently it does, and it's pie-centric. This Kiwi-owned store sells six types of meat pie (one made from real New Zealand beef) and three vegetarian types (we like the Three P's—pumpkin, sweet potato, and paprika). One large table is available if you want to eat your pies in the store, but you can also take them across the street to Sarphatipart.

▶ ⓕ Tram #3 or 25 to 2e Van der Helstraat. Walk 1 block south, away from the park. Von Ostadestraat is on the right. ⓢ Pies €3. ☼ Open Tu-Sa 9am-5:30pm.

JODENBUURT AND PLANTAGE

▨ Eetkunst Asmara

ERITREAN $$

Jonas Daniel Meijerplein 8

☎020 627 10 02

Jodenbuurt started out as a neighborhood of immigrants, and this East African restaurant is a testament to the area's continuing diversity. The menu consists of varieties of delicately spiced meat and vegetables, all served with delicious *injera*, a traditional spongy, slightly tangy bread. Each dish is accompanied by an assortment of lentils and other veggies, so one entree could feed two people. This is one of the best values around and a nice break from Amsterdam's unending parade of sandwiches.

▶ 🚋 Tram #9 or 14 or Ⓜ️Waterlooplein. Walk down Waterlooplein and turn right onto Wesperstraat. Jonas Daniel Mieijerplein is on the right, 1 street after the Jewish Historical Museum. ⓢ Entrees €9.50-11.50. Beer €1.50. ⓘ Open daily 6-11pm.

Plancius   CAFE, SANDWICHES, FRENCH $$

Plantage Kerklaan 61A

☎020 330 94 69; www.restaurantplancius.nl

Right across from the zoo, Plancius is a stylish one-stop shop for everything from breakfast to after-dinner drinks. The menu rotates seasonally, but lunch always offers creative spins on the traditional sandwich, while dinner tends more toward formal French fare like lamb shank and shrimp croquettes.

▶ 🚋 Tram #9 or 14 to Plantage Kerklaan. ⓢ Sandwiches €2.50-8.50. Appetizers €8. Entrees €15-19. ⓘ Open daily 11am-11pm. Lunch menu served until 6pm.

Soep en Zo   SOUP $

Jodenbreestraat 94A

☎020 422 22 43; www.soupenzo.nl

This small outpost of an Amsterdam chain serves fresh soups and a few salads. Soups come with bread and toppings like coriander and cheese. Take advantage of their outside patio when the weather's nice.

▶ 🚋 Tram #9 or 14 or Ⓜ️Waterlooplein. ⓢ Soups €3-7. ⓘ Open M-F 11am-8pm, Sa-Su noon-7pm.

Nightlife

Experiencing Amsterdam's nightlife is an essential part of visiting the city. Sure, you can go to the Rijksmuseum and see a dozen Rembrandts, but there's nothing like stumbling out of a bar at 5am and seeing the great man staring down at you from his pedestal in the middle of Rembrandtplein. That square and its debaucherous cousin, Leidseplein, have all the glitzy clubs, rowdy tourist bars, and live DJs you could ever hope for. For a mellower night out, *bruin cafes* are cafe-pub combinations populated by old Dutch men or hipster students, depending on which neighborhood you're in. The closer you get to the Red Light District, the fewer locals you find, the more British bros on bachelor party trips you're forced to interact with. GLBT venues are a very visible and prominent part of Amsterdam's nightlife, and it's worth bearing in mind that in this city famous for tolerance, virtually every bar and club is GLBT-friendly.

NL20 is a free publication that lists the week's happenings—it's only in Dutch, but it's pretty easy to decipher the names of clubs and DJs. You can find it outside most stores, supermarkets, and tobacco shops. The English-language *Time Out Amsterdam* provides monthly calendars of nightlife, live music, and other events. It can be purchased at newsstands and bookstores.

Budget Nightlife

Nightlife in Amsterdam is world famous. For a reason. This city is packed with enough bars and clubs of enough different varieties that there's no need for you to ever pay a cover, or even for a beer over €4. Be careful with some of the big clubs on Leidseplein and Remembrandtplein, though, as they can charge moderate covers and often change the price from day to day. But the numerous bars and *bruin cafes* tend to offer drinks much cheaper than you'll find them pretty much anywhere else in Europe.

OUDE ZIJD

Though the Oude Zijd is a little tamer at night than certain nearby neighborhoods, its close proximity to the Red Light District ensures consistent energy and some revelling tourists, especially along **Zeedijk.** If you're looking for a place to grab a drink here, both Zeedijk and **Nieuwmarkt** are lined with pubs and cafe-bars. Follow the rainbow flags to find a smattering of ▼**GLBT** bars in the northern part of Zeedijk, near Centraal Station.

Cafe de Engelbewaarder   BAR
Kloveniersburgwal 59
☎020 625 37 72; www.cafe-de-engelbewaarder.nl

The "Guardian Angel" Cafe takes its (exclusively) Belgian beer selection pretty seriously—and so should you. Located on the first floor of a canal house with a handsome, candle-lit seating area by the water, it's the perfect place to converse with artsy young locals. Despite the hipness, welcoming bartenders will gladly help you find the perfect drink. The walls inside are postered with advertisements for local goings-on that will bring you up to speed on all that's, well, going on.

▶ ✝ Ⓜ Nieuwmarkt. *i* Live jazz Su 4:30pm. Occasional art showings; check website for details. Ⓢ Beer from €3. 🕘 Open M-Th 11am-1am, F-Sa 11am-3am, Su 11am-1am.

Het Elfde Gebod   BAR
Zeedijk 5
☎020 622 35 77; www.hetelfdegebod.com

For a country that produces so much beer, the Dutch can be surprisingly unpatriotic in their selections. Het Elfde Gebod is another all-Belgian-beer affair, this time with seven on tap and over 50 in bottles (many of which come served in their own special glasses). Don't worry if you're overwhelmed by the choices; the knowledgeable bartenders are happy to provide recommendations. The bar gets crowded on weekend nights with jolly, well-dressed locals.

▶ # At the beginning of Zeedijk, near Centraal Station. ⓢ Beer from €3. Wine and spirits from €4. ⓩ Open M 5pm-1am, W-Su 3pm-1am.

Cafe de Jaren BAR
Nieuwe Doelenstraat 20-22
☎020 625 57 71; www.cafedejaren.nl

Popular with locals and tourists alike, Cafe de Jaren has an expansive interior and a two-tiered terrace overlooking the Amstel. It seems to be trying hard to be the coolest place in town, so it looks a lot more expensive than it is.

▶ # Tram #4, 9, 16, 24, or 25 to Muntplein. Cross the Amstel and walk ½ a block. ⓢ Beer from €2.50. Wine from €3. Also serves lunch and dinner €15-20. ⓩ Open M-Th 9:30am-1am, F-Sa 9:30am-2am, Su 9:30am-1am.

Cafe "Oost-West" BAR
Zeedijk 85
☎020 422 70 80

The Cafe "Oost-West" prides itself on being an old-fashioned pub where the jokes flow as freely as the booze. The music is unabashedly cheesy and often hilarious (we particularly enjoyed the Dutch techno cover of "Sweet Caroline"), which is just how the slightly rowdy crowd of older locals—often dressed in similarly ridiculous fashion—likes it.

▶ # ⓂNieuwmarkt. ⓢ Beer from €2.50. ⓩ Open M-Th 11am-1am, F-Sa 11am-3am, Su 11am-1am.

RED LIGHT DISTRICT

Ah, the Red Light District at night. Most of the neon glow bathes **Oudezijds Achterburgwal** and the nearby alleyways. Farther over on **Warmoesstraat,** you can still get a tinge of the lascivious luminescence but will find fewer sex-related establishments. Especially on weekends, the whole area is filled with slow-moving crowds of predominantly male tourists. Despite getting very busy, the hotel bars on Warmoesstraat and Oudezijds Voorburgwal can be fun places to mingle with fellow backpackers. Despite police frequently strolling through, the area can turn into a meeting place for dealers and junkies late on weekends.

Wynand Fockink BAR
Pijlsteeg 31
☎020 639 26 95; www.wynand-fockink.nl

Many people avoid small alleyways in the Red Light District for fear of up-close-and-personal contact with a red-lit window, but this one holds a unique draw—an over-300-year-old distillery and tasting room that makes the best *jenever* in the city. Perfect for day-drinking, Wynand Fockink has no music, no flatscreen TV, and not even any chairs: just rows of bottles on creaking shelves behind the small bar. Dozens of liquors are available, with flavorings like cinnamon, rose petals, bergamot, and strawberry. Most are complex blends with names like "Forget Me Not" and "The Bride's Tears," which often come with humorous histories. With as much focus on educating as getting crunk, this bar promises to answer all your burning questions about how the drinks are made—just ask the bartender or take a tour of the distillery.

▶ ✱ From Dam Sq., walk down Dam to Oudezijds Voorburgwal, make the 1st left, and turn left onto Pijlsteeg. ⓢ Spirits from €2.50. ⏲ Open daily 3-9pm. Tours in English Sa 12:30pm.

Durty Nelly's Pub IRISH PUB
Warmoesstraat 115-117
☎020 638 01 25; www.durtynellys.nl

Right underneath Durty Nelly's Hostel, this pub attracts backpackers from upstairs, students from around the world, and drunkards from the official Red Light District pub crawl. There's plenty to keep you entertained, from watching international sports on the TVs to playing pool, foosball, and darts yourself. The atmosphere is fun-loving and rowdy, making it a great place for a pint or six. Durty Nelly's also serves standard pub food, including full Irish breakfast (which, big surprise, includes Guinness).

▶ ✱ From Centraal Station, go south on Damrak, turn right onto Brugsteeg, and turn onto Warmoesstraat. *i* Strict no-smoking policy (tobacco or otherwise). ⓢ Beer from €2. ⏲ Open M-Th 8am-1am, F-Sa 8am-3am, Su 8am-1am.

Cafe Aen't Water
BAR

Oudezijds Voorburgwal 2A

☎020 652 06 18

Smack in the middle of the two busiest Red Light District drags, you'll be surprised by how relaxed you feel and how much Dutch you hear in Cafe Aen't Water. The drunkest and loudest of the Euro-tripping backpackers have been weeded out, making for a casual, quiet atmosphere. The large outdoor patio, which hugs a bend in the canal, is a perfect spot for sipping and people-watching.

▶ ⁂ From Centraal Station, turn left onto Prins Hendrikkade, and right onto Nieuwebrugsteeg. Continue straight as it becomes Oudezijds Voorburgwal. Ⓢ Beer from €2. ⓘ Open M-Th noon-1am, F-Sa noon-3am, Su noon-1am.

Club Winston
CLUB

Warmoesstraat 129

☎020 625 39 12; www.winston.nl

One of the largest and hippest of the many hostel bars and clubs on the block, Winston fills up with tireless dancers. There's also a lounge area across the dance floor, but people tend to stay on their feet. DJs spin everything from rock and metal to indie pop and hip hop—whatever people will get down to. Live acts sometimes play earlier in the evening; check their website for the schedule.

▶ ⁂ From Centraal Station, go south on Damrak, turn right onto Brugsteeg, and left onto Warmoesstraat. Ⓢ Cover for live shows varies by event, usually around €5. Beer from €2.50. ⓘ Hours vary by event, but usually open 9pm-4am.

Getto
GLBT-FRIENDLY, BAR

Warmoesstraat 51

☎020 421 51 51; www.getto.nl

A fun, everyone's-welcome cocktail bar crossed with a diner, Getto offers a phenomenal drink menu featuring homemade infused vodka (flavors range from vanilla to cucumber). The sedate atmosphere of this GLBT-friendly bar doesn't quite live up to its claims to "put the Cock in Cocktail."

▶ ⁂ From Centraal Station, go south on Damrak, turn right onto Brugsteeg, and left onto Warmoesstraat. *i* DJ party Su from 5pm, includes special cocktail deals. Ⓢ Cocktails from €6; happy hour €4.50. ⓘ Open Tu-Th 4pm-1am, F-Sa 4pm-2am, Su 4pm-midnight. Happy hour Tu-Sa 5-7pm.

NIEUWE ZIJD

The Nieuwe Zijd has some decent nightlife, but it's not very concentrated. **Spuistraat** is the place to go for artsier cafes and bars, while **Dam Square** and **Rokin** are lined with larger, rowdier pubs. The small streets in the southern part of the neighborhood are home to good beer bars and a couple of energetic clubs. However, with fewer people around, it can feel a little less safe at night than the jam-packed Leidesplein and Red Light District.

Prik
BAR, CLUB, GLBT

Spuistraat 109

☎020 320 00 02; www.prikamsterdam.nl

Voted both best bar and best gay bar in Amsterdam on multiple occasions, Prik attracts a mostly male crowd. Its atmosphere is about as light and fun as its name ("bubble" in Dutch—get your minds out of the gutter, English speakers). Come for cocktail specials all day Thursday and on Sunday evenings, or to hear DJs spin pop, house, and disco classics on the weekends.

▶ Tram #1, 2, 5, or 14 to Dam/Paleisstraat. Walk down Paleisstraat and turn right onto Spuistraat. Beer from €2. Cocktails from €6. Open M-Th 4pm-1am, F-Sa 4pm-3am, Su 4pm-1am. Kitchen open until 11pm.

Jenever Fever

Amsterdam may be famous for a certain kind of herbal intoxication, but don't let the siren call of coffeeshops prevent you from trying another one of Holland's delights: jenever. A juniper-based alcohol and ancestor of gin, jenever was first sold as a medicine, and then took off as a different kind of remedy once people figured out it tasted good and got you drunk.

Nowadays, some locals swear by a quick two shots of chilled jenever to get you ready for a night on the town. A more common method of imbibing it is a *kopstoot* ("headbutt"), which is a shot of jenever followed by a pint of beer. Most Dutch bars will have one or two generic jenever brands, but for a real authentic selection, head to the centuries-old distillery Wynand Fockink (Pijlsteeg 31-43 ☎020 639 26 95; www.wynand-fockink.nl) in the Red Light District.

🍸 Belgique
BAR

Gravenstraat 2

☎020 625 19 74; www.cafe-belgique.nl

If you can muscle your way through to the bar—it tends to be packed in here, even on weekdays—you'll be rewarded by a choice of eight draft beers and dozens more Belgian and Dutch brews in bottles. "But I'm in the Netherlands," you say, "should I really be at a bar called 'Belgium'?" Be quiet and enjoy your beer.

▶ 🚋 From Dam Sq., walk down Zoutsteeg. The bar is behind the Nieuwe Kerk, in between Nieuwendijk and Nieuwezijds Voorburgwal. ⓢ Beer from €2.50. ⓘ Open daily 2pm-1am.

🍸 Dansen bij Jansen
CLUB

Handboogstraat 11-13

☎020 620 17 79; www.dansenbijjansen.nl

A student-only club, Dansen bij Jansen attracts students from the nearby University of Amsterdam as well as backpackers from local hostels. The music on the crowded dance floor is a slightly cheesy mix of Top 40, R and B, and disco. Upstairs, another bar offers a range of electronic music.

▶ 🚋 Tram #1, 2, or 5 to Koningsplein. Cross the canal, walk up Heiligeweg, and turn left onto Handboogstraat. *i* Must have a student ID or be accompanied by someone who does. ⓢ Cover M-W €2; Th-Sa €5. Beer from €2. ⓘ Open M-Th 11pm-4am, F-Sa 11pm-5am.

🍸 Bitterzoet
BAR, CLUB

Spuistraat 2

☎020 421 23 18; www.bitterzoet.nl

Not as reliably popular as the larger clubs to the south, Bitterzoet is one of the best parties you can find this close to Centraal Station. The crowd is mostly young people jamming to a steady mix of dance, bouncy house, smooth reggae, classic hip hop, and occasional live acts. There's a simple dance room with a cool balcony and smoking room upstairs, creating a generally unpretentious atmosphere.

▶ 🚋 From Centraal Station, walk down Martelaarsgracht, which becomes Hekelweg and then Spuistraat. ⓢ Cover €5-8. Beer from €2. ⓘ Open M-Th 8pm-3am, F-Sa 8pm-4am, Su 8pm-3am.

Gollem
BAR

Raamsteeg 4

☎020 676 71 17; www.cafegollem.nl

This is not a bar for the indecisive. Beer aficionados from all across the city (and the world) flock to Gollem's slightly Gothic interior for the specialty brews. Way back in the '70s, this was one of the first cafes in Amsterdam to serve now-trendy Belgian beers. Nowadays, the bar offers over 200 varieties, with eight on tap. You can find Trappist ales, fruit lambics, doubles, triples—pretty much anything they make in Belgium with yeast and hops. They even have the famed **Westvleteren,** made by reclusive monks in incredibly small batches and only sold at the monastery itself.

▶ Tram #1, 2, or 5 to Spui/Nieuwezijds Voorburgwal. Walk up Spui and turn left onto Raamsteeg. ⓢ Beer from €2.50. Open M-F 4pm-1am, Sa-Su 2pm-2am.

The Tara
IRISH PUB

Rokin 85-89

☎020 421 26 54; www.thetara.com

This Irish pub is large enough to be called a complex. The Tara keeps multiple bars running, so the Guinness flows all night long. Different parts of the building have different themes—go from a hunting lodge to a downtown lounge without even stepping outside. It still attracts enough people for the tourists to be spilling out into the streets. Come here if you're determined to avoid any semblance of local culture.

▶ Tram #4, 9, 14, 16, 24, or 25 to the Spui/Rokin stop. Walk a few blocks up Rokin. The Tara is on the right. ⓢ Beer from €2.70. Open M-Th 10am-1am, F-Sa 10am-3am, Su 11am-1am.

Club NL
CLUB

Nieuwezijds Voorburgwal 169

☎020 622 75 10; www.clubnl.nl

Club NL is a swanky lounge club with a surprisingly low cover. Patrons are slinkily dressed, and we advise you to spruce up a bit before trying to get in, especially later on weekend nights. Music goes from ambient house to more energetic dance tunes; check their website for guest DJ appearances. The carefully crafted cocktail menu is just as image-conscious as the club itself, with delicious results.

▶ Tram #1, 2, 5 or 14 to Dam/Paleisstraat. Walk east down Rozengracht and then right onto Nieuwezijds Voorburgwal. Club NL is south of the stop on Nieuwezijds Voorburgwal. ⓢ Cover F-Sa €5. Beer from €2.50. Cocktails from €8. Open M-Th 10pm-3am, F-Sa 10pm-4am, Su 10pm-3am.

SCHEEPVAARTBUURT

Nightlife in Scheepvaartbuurt isn't exactly happening. After dark, those who do stick around tend to congregate in the coffeeshops on **Haarlemmerstraat**. However, there are a few pleasant places to stop for a quiet drink.

Dulac   BAR
Haarlemmerstraat 118
☎020 624 42 65; www.restaurantdulac.nl

This bar is popular with local and international students (maybe the 50% student discount on food helps with that). The exterior kind of blends into the background of Haarlemmerstraat, but follow the young Dutch kids to find it. You'll know you're in the right place if you find crazy sculptures and many miscellaneous objects inside. There's a nice garden terrace in the back.

▶ ⁂ From Centraal Station, turn right, cross the Singel, and walk down Haarlemmerstraat. ⓢ Beer from €2.50. Entrees €10-18. ⓩ Open M-Th 3pm-1am, F 3pm-3am, Sa 12pm-3am, Su 12pm-1am.

CANAL RING WEST

The Canal Ring West doesn't go wild after sunset, but the pubs along the water are great places to grab a cheap beer and befriend some locals.

De Prins   BAR
Prinsengracht 124
☎020 624 93 82; www.deprins.nl

De Prins attracts artsy types, young locals, and savvy tourists with its classic *bruin cafe* atmosphere. An extensive lunch and dinner menu complements the broad drink selection, which includes five beers on tap. Enjoy your brew at the canal-side seating or inside the wooden interior, which inexplicably features portraits of Al Pacino along with the usual pictures of Queen Beatrix.

▶ ⁂ Tram #13, 14, or 17 to Westermarkt. 2 blocks up Prinsengracht, on the far side. ⓢ Beer €2-3.50. Liquor €3.50-5. ⓩ Open daily 10am-1am. Kitchen closes at 10pm.

Thirsty Dogg   BAR
Oude Leliestraat 9
☎064 512 22 72

A small bar in the Nine Streets that puts the extra "g" in

"dogg," Thirsty Dogg is popular with young locals and the type of tourist who didn't come to Amsterdam to see art museums. The bar has an excellent selection of liquor, including six types of absinthe. During the week, the bartender dictates the music selection, which tends toward heavy hip hop; on some weekend nights a live DJ brings in trip hop and dubstep. Some travelers consider Thirsty Dogg a marijuana-friendly environment.

▶ ✆ Tram #13, 14, or 17 to Westermarkt. Walk down Raadhuisstraat, make a left onto Herengracht, and then a right onto Oude Leliestraat. ⓢ Beer €2.50. Wine €3. Absinthe €4. ⏰ Open M-Th 4pm-1am, F-Sa 4pm-3am, Su 4pm-1am.

Cafe Brandon   BAR
Keizersgracht 157
☎065 434 71 36

The owners of this tiny bar took an 18-year hiatus when they won the lottery... twice in one year. Maybe they blew all the money, because Cafe Brandon has now reopened, much to the joy of the locals who pack it to the brim on weekends. A pool table fills the back room, and the walls are covered in Dutch memorabilia. Comfy outdoor seating includes benches with large cushions, but when this place fills up, most people just stand around looking hip.

▶ ✆ Tram #13, 14, or 17 to Westermarkt. 1 block up Keizersgracht, on the corner with Leliegracht. ⓢ Beer €2.50. ⏰ Open M-Th 11am-1am, F-Sa 11am-3am, Su 11am-1am.

CENTRAL CANAL RING

With the meccas of Leidseplein and Rembrandtplein at its corners, the Central Canal Ring doesn't have much in the way of its own nightlife. Given their proximity to the larger squares, **Spiegelgracht** and **Utrechtsestraat** house most of the neighborhood bars, including some decent places to have a quiet drink.

Cafe Brecht   CAFE, BAR
Weteringschans 157
☎020 627 22 11; www.cafebrecht.nl

Cafe Brecht delivers everything you'd expect from a place named after a Marxist poet, playwright, and theorist (Bertolt Brecht). The cafe prides itself on its beer, which comes from an old Czech brewery, and most of the ingredients on the daytime soup-and-sandwich menu are organic and local. Brecht hosts free poetry readings and live music on the first Monday of each month. Though we aren't sure what exactly it has to do with a bar or German art, you can get a haircut here on Wednesdays.

▶ 🚋 Tram #7 or 10 to Spiegelgracht. Walk down Weteringschans and it's on the right. ⓢ Beer from €2. ⓘ Open M-Th noon-1am, F-Sa noon-3am, Su noon-1am. Poetry nights start at 10:30pm.

Mankind

GLBT-FRIENDLY, BAR

Weteringstraat 60

☎020 638 47 55; www.mankind.nl

In a quiet spot just a few blocks from Leidseplein and the Rijksmuseum, Mankind is an ideal bar to grab an afternoon or evening beer. Two outdoor patios, one facing Weteringstraat and the other adjacent to the canal, allow you to people-watch by land or by sea. Mankind draws local regulars but also caters to tourists with an extremely friendly staff happy to give recommendations. Mankind serves the usual menu of Dutch bar snacks (*bitterballen, tostis,* etc.), as well as a more substantial meal-of-the-day. Though it's advertised as GLBT-friendly, the bar's crowd is not exclusively gay.

▶ 🚋 Tram #7 or 10 to Spiegelgracht. Walk down Weteringschans and turn left. ⓢ Beer from €2. ⓘ Open M-Sa noon-11pm. Kitchen closes at 8pm.

LEIDSEPLEIN

"Leidseplein" roughly translates to "more diverse nightlife per sq. ft. than anywhere else in the city" (don't listen to anyone who feeds you a story about how it means something to do with a road to the city of Leiden). Some native Amsterdammers scoff at this area, considering it a sea of drunken British and American tourists. But the bars that cater to these liquored-up crowds are primarily confined to the Korte and Lange Leidsedwarsstraats. The rest of the area hosts some very hip and friendly bars as well as a few terrific nightclubs. You can also find several bastions of incredible live music scattered throughout the neighborhood, and, unless you're going to a big-name event at **Paradiso** or **Melkweg,** prices are extremely reasonable. Many establishments are just as full of locals as they are of tourists. If you want to be one of the revelers that gives the Leidseplein its bad name, check out the Leidseplein Pub Crawl (promoters lurk in the main square all day long).

Leidseplein

🏷 Weber   BAR
Marnixstraat 397
☎020 622 99 10

Tremendously popular with young locals and a few stylish tourists, Weber is the place to be. Come early or late (after people have departed for the clubs) if you want to get a seat on a weekend night. Frilly red lampshades and vintage pornographic art give the place a cheeky bordello feel, complemented by jazzy French pop. But don't be fooled: this bar steers clear of the tawdriness that plagues so much of Amsterdam's nightlife.

▶ 🚋 Tram #1, 2, 5, 6, 7, or 10 to Leidseplein. Walk south of the main square and make a right onto Marnixstraat. 💲 Beer from €2.50. Spirits from €4. 🕐 Open M-Th 8pm-3am, F-Sa 8pm-4am, Su 8pm-3am.

🏷 Paradiso   CLUB, CONCERT VENUE
Weteringschans 6-8
☎020 626 45 21; www.paradiso.nl

You can have a very good Friday in this former church. Paradiso began in 1968 as the "Cosmic Relaxation Center Paradiso," and its laid-back vibe (at least, as laid-back as you get in one of the city's most popular clubs) keeps this place true to its roots. The club generally attracts less well-known artists than nearby Melkweg, though it has played host to big names like Wu-Tang Clan and Lady Gaga. Check out the live music every day and club nights five nights per week—including *Noodlanding!* ("emergency landing!"), a party with "alternative dance hits" on Thursdays.

▶ 🚋 Tram #1, 2, 5, 6, 7, or 10 to Leidseplein. Take a left onto Weteringschans. 💲 Concert tickets €5-20, plus €3 monthly membership fee. Cover for club nights €5-20. 🕐 Hours vary by event; check website for details.

🏷 Sugar Factory   CLUB
Lijnbaansgracht 238
☎020 626 50 06; www.sugarfactory.nl

Billing itself as a *nachttheater,* Sugar Factory is, at its core, just a very sweet place to dance. Music is the main focus here: it tends to outshine that of larger clubs nearby, and includes house, electro, and "club jazz." Live music and DJs are accompanied by mind-bending video displays and dancers. The sizeable dance floor fills with a mix of young Dutch hipsters, older locals, and clusters of tourists. Check the website for upcoming events, though it's safe to assume that there's something going on Friday and Saturday from midnight to 5am.

- 🚊 Tram #1, 2, 5, 6, 7, or 10 to Leidseplein. Turn down the small street to the left of the Stadsschouwburg theater. ⓢ Cover varies depending on event; usually €8-12. Beer from €3. Cocktails €6.50. ⓘ Hours vary depending on event; check website for details.

🅜 Melkweg   CLUB, CONCERT VENUE
Lijnbaansgracht 234A
☎020 531 81 81; www.melkweg.nl

The name translates to "milky way"—a pun on the fact that this cultural center is housed in an old milk factory. One of Amsterdam's legendary nightspots and concert venues, Melkweg hosts rock, punk, pop, indie, reggae, electronic… basically any type of music that exists in the big Milky Way has probably been played in this little one. Popular events sell out quickly, so keep an eye on the website if you're planning a visit. Club nights follow the concerts on Friday and Saturday. The building is also home to theater performances, photography exhibits, and a restaurant.

- 🚊 Tram #1, 2, 5, 6, 7, or 10 to Leidseplein. Turn down the small street to the left of the Stadsschouwburg theater. ⓢ Tickets €10-30, plus €3.50 monthly membership fee. ⓘ Hours vary depending on event, but concerts usually start at 8 or 9pm. Clubbing gets going around 11pm or midnight.

De Pieper   BRUIN CAFE
Prinsengracht 424
☎020 626 47 75

One of Amsterdam's oldest cafes, De Pieper lives in a building that's been around since the 17th century. The low ceilings and dark paneling reflect the building's age, but De Pieper also makes quirky nods to modernity, with strings of fairy lights and posters from performances at nearby venues. This is a place to escape from the bustle of the Leidseplein in a dark, subdued *bruin cafe* (though who comes to Leidseplein for that?).

- 🚊 Tram #1, 2, or 5 to Prinsengracht or #7 or 10 to Raamplein. At the corner of Prinsengracht and Leidsegracht. ⓢ Beer from €2.50. ⓘ Open M-Th 11am-1am, F-Sa 11am-3am.

Bourbon Street   BLUES CLUB
Leidsekruisstraat 6-8
☎020 623 34 40

One of the better touristy joints in the square, Bourbon Street is a bustling home to nightly live blues, soul, and funk shows. The walls are packed with memorabilia and photos from past events. They host jam nights on Monday, Tuesday, and

Sunday, where all are welcome to bring their own instruments and play along—these tend to be high-quality, since if you're willing to haul your gear to the Leidseplein, you're probably pretty good.)

▶ 🚋 Tram #1, 2, 5, 6, 7, or 10 to Leidseplein. Make a right onto Korte Leidsedwarsstraat and Leidsekruisstraat is on the left. ⑤ Cover varies, up to €5. Beer from €3. ⓘ Open M-Th 10pm-4am, F-Sa 10pm-5am, Su 10pm-4am. Music starts M-Th 10:30pm, F-Sa 11pm, Su 10:30pm.

Punto Latino
CLUB, SALSA

Lange Leidsedwarsstraat 35
☎020 420 22 35

Punto Latino is a small salsa club that's popular on the weekends for fiery Latin music and dancing. It attracts a crowd of young tourists and older locals, many of Spanish or Latin origin.

▶ 🚋 Tram #1, 2, 5, 6, 7, or 10 to Leidseplein. ⑤ Beer €2.50. ⓘ Open daily 11pm-4am.

REMBRANDTPLEIN

Rembrandtplein *is* its nightlife. Yeah, there's a pretty sweet statue of Rembrandt in the middle of this square, but if you were interested in the man himself, then you would be at one of Amsterdam's many fine museums, none of which can be found here. This is home to the art of looking good and getting down, not the art of the Dutch Renaissance. The square itself is lined with massive bars and clubs, while the streets that fan out from it are home to smaller establishments. **Reguliersdwarstraat,** known as "the gayest street in Amsterdam," is lined with a diverse array of gay bars and clubs, though many can be found on neighboring streets as well. Whatever you're looking for in nightlife can be found here: Irish pub, sleek bar, chic club, grungy dive, gay cafe, tourist dance party. Just walk around until you hear some music that you like. Rembrandtplein is conveniently serviced by night buses #355, 357, 359, 361, and 363; taxis also loiter around the main square at all hours.

📰 Studio 80
CLUB

Rembrandtplein 17
www.studio-80.nl

Many swear that Studio 80 *is* Amsterdam nightlife. A grungier alternative to the more polished clubs around Rembrandtplein, Studio 80 is extremely popular with students and young Dutch hipsters, and with good reason—the emphasis here is squarely on good music and good dancing. This is also where young Amsterdammers flock to have a wild night out on the town, and where in-the-know tourists come to get a taste of the action.

- ▶ 🚋 Tram #9 or 14 to Rembrandtplein. The entrance is next to Escape (see below), under the large balcony. ⓢ Cover depends on the night, usually €6-10. Beer €2.50. ⓘ Open W-Th 11pm-3:30am, F-Sa 11pm-5am.

Vive la Vie
BAR, GLBT

Amstelstraat 7

☎020 624 01 14; www.vivelavie.net

This long-established lesbian bar draws a diverse crowd of mostly young women and a few of their male friends. The atmosphere is refreshingly unpretentious, focusing on dancing and having a good time. The excellent drink selection includes the Clit on Fire shot (€4). Music ranges from indie rock and bluesy country in the early evening, toward more dance and hip hop as the night progresses.

- ▶ 🚋 Tram #9 or 14 to Rembrandtplein. ⓢ Beer from €2.20. Spirits from €3. ⓘ Open M-Th 4pm-3am, F-Sa 4pm-4am, Su 4pm-3am.

Escape
CLUB

Rembrandtplein 11

☎020 622 11 11; www.escape.nl

This is Amsterdam's biggest club, with a capacity for thousands. Although it may no longer be the hottest spot in town, it still draws reliably large crowds and excellent DJs. Escape is an institution—its hulking form dominates Rembrandtplein—and it has the cover and drink prices to match. The main dance floor features a massive stage (VIP area behind the DJ) and platforms scattered throughout for those brave enough to take the dancing spotlight. Upstairs, there's a lounge, another dance space, and a balcony from which to observe the bacchanalia below. The music varies depending on the DJ but generally tends toward house, electro, and trance. The crowd is a mix of droves of tourists and young-to-middle-aged Dutch. Lines can get long on weekends after 1am: some suggest that upping your style will increase your chances of getting in.

- ▶ 🚋 Tram #9 or 14 to Rembrandtplein. Almost impossible to miss, under the huge TV screen. ⓢ Cover €5-16. Beer from €2.60 (in a tiny glass). Spirits €3.80-5.80. ⓘ Open Th 11pm-4am, F-Sa 11pm-5am, Su 11pm-4:30am.

De Duivel
BAR

Reguliersdwarsstraat 87

☎020 626 61 84; www.deduivel.nl

Amsterdam's premier hip-hop joint has attracted the likes of

Public Enemy, Cypress Hill, and Ghost Face, but even without famous guests, De Duivel remains a nighttime favorite, with expert DJs drawing a diverse group of music-lovers. The intimidating stained-glass devil that gives the bar its name overlooks the small dance floor, but most patrons seem to be more interested in chilling and nodding their heads to the music than in showcasing their dance moves.

▶ Tram #9 or 14 to Rembrandtplein. ⑤ Beer €2.50. ⌚ Open M-Th 10pm-3am, F-Sa 10pm-4am, Su 10pm-3am.

Montmartre
BAR, GLBT

Halvemaansteeg 17

☎020 625 55 65; www.cafemontmartre.nl

A sinfully luxurious Garden of Eden-inspired interior provides the backdrop for this popular spot, regularly voted the best gay bar in Amsterdam. The crowd is dominated by gay men, but all are welcome. As the night wears on, the dancing heats up to Euro and American pop and bouncy disco. Special theme nights spice up each day of the week.

▶ Tram #9 or 14 to Rembrandtplein. Off of the northwest corner of the square. ⑤ Beer from €2.50. Liquor from €3.50. ⌚ Open M-Th 5pm-1am, F-Sa 5pm-3am, Su 5pm-1am.

Lellebel
BAR, GLBT

Utrechtstraat 4

☎020 427 51 39; www.lellebel.nl

Outrageous drag queens preside over this bar just off the square, where the decor is as campy as the costumes. Lellebel plays host to a variety of theme nights—karaoke, "Transgender Cafe," Miss Lellebel contests, and a Eurovision party, to name a few—and attracts a mostly older, gay male crowd.

▶ Tram #9 or 14 to Rembrandtplein. Just off the southeast corner of the square. *i* Karaoke Tu. "Transgender Cafe" W. Red Hot Salsa Night Th. ⑤ Beer €2.50. ⌚ Open M-Th 8pm-3am, F-Sa 8pm-4am, Su 8pm-3am.

JORDAAN

Nightlife in the Jordaan is much more relaxed than in Leidseplein or Nieuwe Zijd, but that doesn't mean it's not popular or busy. Establishments tend more toward cafe-bars or local pubs than clubs, though some excellent music can be found in the neighborhood's southern stretches. If you're looking to seriously mingle with the locals, try one of the lively-on-weekends places along **Lijnbaansgracht** and **Noordermarkt**.

◪ Festina Lente BAR
Looiersgracht 40B
☎020 638 14 12; www.cafefestinalente.nl

Looking something like a bar stuck in the middle of an elegant vintage living room, this spot is enduringly popular with fun and cultured young Amsterdammers who want to "make haste, slowly." Bookshelves line the walls, and games of chess and checkers are readily available—if you can find a spot to play. Poetry contests and live concerts are held often (check the website for details). The menu features *lentini*, small Mediterranean dishes, and an astonishing selection of bruschettas (on homemade bread!). No wonder it's always so crowded.

▶ 🚋 Tram #7, 10, or 17 to Elandsgracht. Go straight on Elandsgracht and turn right onto Hazenstraat; the bar is 2 blocks down on the corner. ⑤ Beer from €2. Wine from €3.30 per glass. ⓘ Open M noon-1am, Tu-Th 10:30am-1am, F-Sa 10:30am-3am, Su noon-1am. Kitchen closes at 10:30pm.

◪ Saarein BRUIN CAFE, GLBT
Elandsstraat 119
☎020 623 49 01; www.saarein.info

A classic *bruin cafe* in the Jordaan tradition but with a GLBT focus, Saarein mainly attracts a local group of older lesbians, but no matter what your gender or orientation, you're sure to have fun. Saarein hosts a variety of events, including a pool competition every Tuesday and a bi-weekly "underground disco party."

▶ 🚋 Tram #7, 10, or 17 to Elandsgracht. Make a left onto Lijnbaansgracht and walk 2 blocks. *i* Free Wi-Fi, and a computer available. ⑤ Beer from €2. ⓘ Open Tu-Th 4pm-1am, F 4pm-2am, Sa noon-2am, Su noon-1am.

't Smalle CAFE, BRUIN CAFE
Egelantiersgracht 12
☎020 623 96 17

't Smalle was founded in 1780 as a spot to taste the products of a nearby *jenever* distillery. It's one of the most revered and popular *bruin cafes* in the city, but be warned: "revered and popular" can manifest itself in the form of stuffy middle-aged people chilling. Enjoy your drink or snacks like "Doritos with sauce" on the airy upper level of the old-fashioned interior, or, if you can get a spot, outside at one of the many tables lining Egelantiersgracht, one of the prettiest canals in Amsterdam.

- ▶ 🚋 Tram #13, 14, or 17 to Westermarkt. Cross Prinsengracht, turn right, and walk a few blocks. ⑤ Beer from €2. Wine and spirits €4-5. ⏰ Open M-Th 10am-1am, F-Sa 10am-2am, Su 10am-1am.

Cafe Chris BAR
Bloemstraat 42
☎020 624 59 42; www.cafechris.nl

Workers building the tower of the nearby Westerkerk used to stop here to pick up (and then probably spend) their paychecks—the bar first opened its doors in 1624, making it the oldest in the Jordaan. Come today to mingle with the local after-work crowd and let the gloomy dark wood interior transport you back in time to an era before electricity and indoor plumbing—okay, maybe not that far back.

- ▶ 🚋 Tram #13, 14, or 17 to Westermarkt. Cross Prinsengracht, make a right, and walk 1 block. ⑤ Beer €3-5. ⏰ Open M-Th 3pm-1am, F-Sa 3pm-2am, Su 3-9pm.

WESTERPARK AND OUD-WEST

Large swathes of this area are dead at night, but you can brush shoulders with the locals for cheap if you know the right spots. Look for posters advertising weekend parties, as many of the establishments here keep irregular hours.

🔖 OT301 CLUB
Overtoom 301
www.ot301.nl

Home to everything even remotely entertaining—a temporary handicrafts store, a cinema, live music, yoga and acrobatic classes, a vegan restaurant, and excellent DJ parties on most weekend nights—OT301 provides an escape from the typical tourist to-do list. The building was occupied by squatting artists in the late '90s, and OT301 eventually became a destination for Amsterdam's hippest residents. A diverse and laid-back crowd congregates for OT301's parties, which feature music ranging from electro house to soul and funk.

- ▶ 🚋 Tram #1 to J. Pieter Heijestraat. *i* Check the website for upcoming events, or just wander in and peruse the decorated handbills. ⑤ Cover €3-5 most nights. ⏰ Hours vary depending on programming; check website for details.

Bike 'n' Beer

Want to drink beer, get to where you want to go, and be ecologically friendly, all at the same time? The Dutch seem to share the same extremely specific desires. The **Beer-Bike Bar** is a creation that allows 10-19 people to sit around a bar as they are pedaled through the streets. The multi-tasking and extremely in-shape bartender serves the drinks as he pedals the contraption.

Recently, there has been some backlash against the drink-while-you-go philosophy because of several accidents involving distracted beer-bikers. Thankfully, these concerns have influenced a new law requiring no more than 30 liters of beer on any bike bar, no matter how many people are riding. That means passengers may only drink half a keg en route to another bar—a tragedy, really.

Pacific Parc
BAR, CONCERT VENUE

Polonceaukade 23

☎020 488 77 78; www.pacificparc.nl

"Industrial honky-tonk" is the best phrase we can think of to describe this large bar on the end of the Westergasfabriek. Iron staircases and a massive stove in one corner recall the building's factory roots, while the cowhide coverings on the window shades will make you feel as if you're home, home on the range. The who-knows-what-the-hell-it's-made-of chandelier has to be seen to be believed. Spread out on plenty of tables and cushioned benches as you enjoy a drink amid a local, late-20s crowd. There's also space for dancing to the blues and old-school country rock. They have live music some nights, beginning at 11pm. Pacific Parc doubles as a restaurant during the day.

▶ 🚋 Tram #10 to Van Limburg Stirumstraat or Van Hallstraat. Either way, walk to the Haarlemmerweg and cross over; it's at the corner of the Westergasfabriek that is farthest from Westerpark. Ⓢ Beer from €2.50. Wine and spirits from €3. ⏰ Open M-Th 11am-1am, F-Sa 11am-3am, Su 11am-11pm.

MUSEUMPLEIN AND VONDELPARK

The museums don't often stay open past 6pm, so there's not much reason to come to Museumplein in the evening. Vondelpark has a handful of spots for grabbing a drink and enjoying the scenery, but if you're looking for a lively night out, you'd best head elsewhere.

Blauwe Theehuis   BAR
Vondelpark 5
☎020 662 02 54; www.blauwetheehuis.nl

This bar looks a bit like a UFO that's just crash-landed on Earth. Alien or not, 't Blawe Theehuis is probably the only bar in the city center where you can drink while surrounded by trees and greenery. Enjoy the view from the large circular patio outside or the terrace above.

▶ ✈ Tram #2 to Jacob Obrechtstraat. Enter Vondelpark, walk straight, cross the footbridge, and you should see the building ahead. Ⓢ Beer from €2.30. Spirits from €2.40. Wine from €3. ⓘ Open M-Th 9am-10:30pm, F-Sa 9am-midnight, Su 9am-10pm.

DE PIJP

De Pijp does laid-back hipster bars with good beer, good food, and good company—and it does them very well.

▨ Chocolate Bar   BAR
1e Van Der Helststraat 62A
☎020 675 76 72; www.chocolate-bar.nl

While most bars in the neighborhood have a cafe vibe, Chocolate Bar is more like a cocktail lounge. The long, glossy bar and seating area peppered with small, chic tables make the place classy. An outdoor patio with couches and picnic tables provides a prime place to survey the De Pijp scene. On weekends, DJs spin laid-back dance tunes inside.

▶ ✈ Tram #16 or 24 to Albert Cuypstraat. Walk 1 block down Albert Cuypstraat and turn right. Ⓢ Beer from €2. Cocktails €7. ⓘ Open M-Th 10am-1am, F-Sa 10am-3am, Su 11am-1am.

Trouw Amsterdam   CLUB
Wibautstraat 127
☎020 463 77 88; www.trouwamsterdam.nl

Housed in the former office building of the newspaper *Trouw*, this complex includes a restaurant, exhibition space, and club. It's gritty, industrial, and extremely popular with local students. The music ranges from dubstep to house and more; check the website for specific events. If you just can't stop partying, you'll be pleased to know they occasionally host after-parties beginning at 6am.

▶ 🚋 Tram #3 or ⓜWibautstraat. Walk a few blocks south on Wibautstraat and watch out for a giant white office building that says "Trouw" on the upper corner. ⓢ Cover €10-17. ⓘ Open F-Sa 10:30pm-5am (sometimes Th and Su as well). Check website for specifics.

Kingfisher BAR

Ferdinand Bolstraat 24

☎020 671 23 95

One of the bars responsible for the initial cool-ification of De Pijp, Kingfisher hasn't let the popularity go to its head. They've got a good selection of international beers and a spacious wood interior. It gets crowded on weekend nights, but on a sunny afternoon you should still be able to grab one of the coveted outside tables.

▶ 🚋 Tram #16 or 24 to Stadhouderskade. Walk 1 block down Ferdinand Bolstraat. ⓢ Beer from €2. ⓘ Open M-Th 11am-1am, F-Sa 11am-3am, Su noon-1am.

JODENBUURT AND PLANTAGE

This is not the neighborhood for rowdy nightlife. If you're looking for a big night out, you'd do better to head to nearby Rembrandtplein or Nieuwmarkt.

🆕 de Sluyswacht BAR

Jodenbreestraat 1

☎020 625 76 11; www.sluyswacht.nl

This tiny, tilting 17th-century building houses the kind of bar you'd expect to find on a lone seacoast, not a bustling street. The outdoor patio sits right above the canal, with giant umbrellas ready in case it starts to rain. When it gets really inclement, the plain wooden interior is invitingly snug. This bar is perfect for day-drinking and people-watching, with a good selection of draft and bottled beers.

▶ 🚋 Tram #9 or 14 or ⓜWaterlooplein. Walk north from the stop and turn left onto Jodenbreestraat. ⓢ Beer €2-4. ⓘ Open M-Th 11:30am-1am, F-Sa 11:30am-3am, Su 11:30am-7pm.

Arts and Culture

Amsterdam offers a whole host of cultural attractions, many of which are very affordable. The music, film, and arts festivals that take place throughout the summer, along with countless top-notch underground music venues, make the city an absolute paradise for art-lovers. In a city where the most cutting-edge photography exhibits are held in a 17th-century canal house, the performing arts in Amsterdam predictably run the gamut from traditional to bizarre. Many establishments provide significant student discounts or rush tickets so that, even on a budget, you can take a trip to the theater or see the famed Concertgebouw, which some say has the best acoustics in the world.

Budget Arts and Culture

When in Amsterdam, you'll find an arts scene that ranges from the underground rap of Odd Future Wolf Gang Kill Them All to Tchaikovsky. Whatever your scene is, remember that discounts, freebies, and the like reward all those who seek them in Amsterdam—whether that be students, last-minute rushers, or just charming customers. Live music is particularly reasonably priced here, and you can sometimes catch a legit act for less than €10.

CLASSICAL MUSIC AND OPERA

Classical music is a strong presence in Amsterdam, thanks to the various high-caliber orchestras and innovative chamber ensembles that call this city home. Churches (especially the **Oude Kerk**) regularly hold organ and choral concerts and are particularly nice in the summer, when a lot of the concert halls close. Use this guide to begin your exploration of Amsterdam's arts scene, but, as with nightlife, keep an eye out for posters advertising upcoming events.

Concertgebouw　　　　MUSEUMPLEIN AND VONDELPARK

Concertgebouwplein 2-6

☎020 573 05 73; www.concertgebouw.nl

Home to the highly renowned **Royal Concertgebouw Orchestra,** this performance space boasts some of the best acoustics in the world. They manage to fit in 900 concerts each year—primarily classical but also some jazz and world music. You can catch rehearsal concerts for free on Wednesdays at 12:30pm during the summer.

▶ ✠ Tram #3, 5, 12, 16, or 24 to Museumplein. *i* Guided tours available. ⑤ Varies by concert, but generally €15-100. ☼ Ticket office open M-F 1-7pm, Sa-Su 10am-7pm.

Muziektheater　　　　JODENBUURT AND PLANTAGE

Waterlooplein 22

☎625 54 55; www.het-muziektheater.nl

This large complex in Jodenbuurt is the best place in Amsterdam to see opera and classical ballet—it's the home turf of both the **Netherlands Opera** and the **Dutch National Ballet.** Muziektheater also hosts performances by visiting companies and some more modern works. Rush tickets are available for students 1½hr. before curtain for the ballet (€10) and opera (€15).

▶ ✠ Ⓜ︎Waterlooplein. ⑤ Most tickets €15-100. ☼ Box office open early Sept-July M-Sa 10am-6pm, Su 11:30am-2:30pm, and before curtain on performance days. Check for information about free summer concerts.

Muziekgebouw aan't IJ　　　　JODENBUURT AND PLANTAGE

Piet Heinkade 1

☎020 788 20 00; www.muziekgebouw.nl

This is the prime spot in the city for cutting-edge classical music. In addition to their main concert hall, performances are also held in a smaller hall that houses a newly renovated, 31-tone Fokker organ. They clearly have the interests of young people at heart, as they set aside a certain number of "Early

Bird" tickets (€10) for those under 30. If you miss out on those, you can still try to get under-30 rush tickets (also €10) 30min. before performances.

▶ 🚊 Tram #25 or 26 to Muziekgebouw Bimhuis. Make a hairpin turn around the small inlet of water to get to the theater. ⓢ Most tickets €18. ⏰ Box office open from mid-Aug to June M-Sa noon-6pm.

LIVE MUSIC

It's not hard to find great live music in Amsterdam. Many local artists tend toward electronic, techno, and house music, but you'll find home-grown bands and international indie, punk, pop, and hip-hop acts as well. Small jazz and blues joints can be found throughout the city. Leidseplein and the Oud-West boast particularly high concentrations of quality venues, ranging from large all-purpose clubs and concert halls to cozy bars and repurposed squats. In the summer, festivals explode in Amsterdam and the surrounding cities, often centered around electronic or reggae (Amsterdam has this thing with reggae, we can't imagine why). Check the websites of major venues, look for posters around the city, and consult the newspapers *NL20* or *Time Out Amsterdam* for the most up-to-date listings.

🏛 De Nieuwe Anita   WESTERPARK AND OUD-WEST
Frederick Hendrikstraat 111
☎064 150 35 12; www.denieuweanita.nl

De Nieuwe Anita's popularity exploded recently when people realized that the cushy room at the front wasn't just some tasteful person's private living room. It's actually a great bar filled with creative and intellectual types with a super-cool music room attached. American and Dutch underground and indie bands draw gangs of young local hipsters, while more diverse crowds show up for cheap movie screenings and readings.

▶ 🚊 Tram #3 to Hugo de Grootplein. Or take tram #10, 13, 14, or 17 to Rozengracht. Head north on Marnixstraat, make the 1st left before the Bloemgracht stop, cross the canal, and make another left at the traffic circle. ⓢ Usually €5-10. ⏰ Hours vary; check website for details.

🏛 Melkweg   LEIDSEPLEIN
Lijnbaansgracht 234A
☎020 531 81 81; www.melkweg.nl

Melkweg is a legendary venue for all kinds of live music as well as clubbing. See the full listing in **Nightlife.**

- ▸ ✇ Tram #1, 2, 5, 6, 7, or 10 to Leidseplein. Turn down the small street to the left of the Stadsschouwburg theater. ⓢ Tickets generally €10-30; €3.50 monthly membership required. ☏ Hours vary, but concerts usually start around 8 or 9pm.

Paradiso
LEIDSEPLEIN

Weteringschans 6-8

☎020 626 45 21; www.paradiso.nl

Paradiso hosts shows by everyone from big-name pop acts to experimental DJs. See the full listing in **Nightlife.**

- ▸ ✇ Tram #1, 2, 5, 6, 7, or 10 to Leidseplein. Take a left onto Weteringschans. ⓢ Tickets usually €5-20; €3 monthly membership required. ☏ Hours vary; check website for details.

Alto
LEIDSEPLEIN

Korte Leidsedwarsstraat 115

☎020 626 32 49; www.jazz-cafe-alto.nl

Amsterdam's most respected jazz joint, Alto is small, dark, and intimate. Look for the giant saxophone outside. With a loyal following and nightly performances by renowned artists, this place fills up quickly, so show up early to get a good seat.

- ▸ ✇ Tram #1, 2, 5, 6, 7, or 10 to Leidseplein. Korte Leidsedwarsstraat is in the corner of the square. ☏ Open M-Th 9pm-3am, F-Sa 9pm-4am, Su 9pm-3am. Music starts daily at 10pm.

Cotton Club
NIEUWE ZIJD

Nieuwmarkt 5

☎020 626 61 92; www.cottonclubmusic.nl

Cotton Club is an old and storied jazz club on the edge of Nieuwmarkt. Come every Saturday between 5 and 8pm to hear free concerts by the house band (often joined by special guests). There are occasionally other shows, but for most of the week this is just a relaxed place to enjoy a drink.

- ▸ ✇ Ⓜ Nieuwmarkt. ⓢ Beer from €2.50. Weekly concerts are free. ☏ Open M-Th noon-1am, F-Sa noon-2am, Su noon-1am.

Maloe Melo
LEIDSEPLEIN

Lijnbaansgracht 163

☎020 420 45 92; www.maloemelo.nl

This small bar with a simple stage seems more like New Orleans than Amsterdam. Maloe Melo is run by a father and son team—the dad sometimes joins performers on the accordion. There's

live music every night and frequent jam sessions throughout the week. This is a good place to hear some decent blues along with a smattering of jazz and country.
- ▶ 🚋 Tram #7, 10, or 17 to Elandsgracht. Walk up the Jordaan side of Lijnbaansgracht a few blocks. 💲 Weekend cover to music room €5-7.50. Beer from €2. 🕑 Open M-Th 9pm-3am, F-Sa 9pm-4am, Su 9pm-3am. Music room opens 10:30pm.

THEATER AND COMEDY

Traditional theater and musicals don't have the same presence in Amsterdam as they do in many other cities. The comedy scene is perhaps more varied and vibrant. For entertainment you can picnic to, don't miss the **Open Air Theater** in Vondelpark in July.

🎭 Boom Chicago   LEIDSEPLEIN
Leidseplein 12
☎020 423 01 01; www.boomchicago.nl

Boom Chicago is the place for extremely popular improv comedy with plenty of audience participation. English-only shows manage to poke fun at Dutch as well, which you'll probably appreciate after spending a while in Amsterdam. Wednesday is student night: up to four students can get in using one regular ticket.
- ▶ 🚋 Tram #1, 2, 5, 7, or 10 to Leidseplein. At the far corner of the square. 💲 Tickets €20-25. 🕑 Most shows begin 8 or 9pm; check website for details.

Comedy Theater   RED LIGHT DISTRICT
Nes 110
☎020 422 27 77; www.comedytheater.nl

The three comedy troupes based here offer standup in both Dutch and English. Comedy Theater sometimes host international guests as well. Open-mic nights take place a few times per month, so start practicing now. Jokes at the expense of Germans will probably go down well.
- ▶ 🚋 Tram #4, 9, 14, 16, 24, or 25 to Spui/Rokin. Cross the canal and make a left onto Nes. 💲 Most tickets up to €20. 🕑 Shows start beween 7:30 and 9pm. Box office open W-Th 5:30-8:30pm, F-Sa 5:30-11:30pm.

Stadsschouwburg   LEIDSEPLEIN
Leidseplein 26
☎020 624 23 11; www.ssba.nl

A prime spot for catching theater in Amsterdam and the base

> ### Surprise Cinema
>
> Pop-ups come in bad (porn ads when your dad looks over your shoulder) and good (birthday cards with $50 stuffed inside) flavors. Cinema41, a pop-up movie theater, definitely falls in the latter category. The smallest cinema in the world, Cinema41 is open to anyone at anytime—just email cinema41@golfstromen.nl to make a reservation. You'll receive an email with the exact location of the theater. The movies vary, but expect to see some classics. At a mere €3, including soda and popcorn, it's a great way to spend a rainy Amsterdam afternoon.

for the **Holland Festival** in June, Stadsschouwburg also hosts opera and dance performances. The attached cafe that spills out onto the Leidseplein is almost as popular as the theater itself.

▶ 🚋 Tram #1, 2, 5, 7, or 10 to Leidseplein. ⓢ Tickets €10-20. 🕑 Box office open M-Sa noon-6pm.

FILM

It's easy to catch a wide variety of old, new, and totally out-there films in Amsterdam. Most English-language movies are screened with Dutch subtitles. Look out for film festivals in the summer, like EYE institute's **North by Northwest.**

📰 EYE Institute   MUSEUMPLEIN AND VONDELPARK
Vondelpark 3
☎020 589 14 00; www.eyefilm.nl

This elegant theater at the edge of Vondelpark mostly shows new indie flicks from around the world. They also play classics, organize retrospectives on important actors and directors, and host occasional exhibits. The institute also has an extensive library, located across the street.

▶ 🚋 Tram #1, 3, or 12 to 1e Con. Huygensstraat/Overtoom. Walk down 1e Con. Huygensstraat, turn right onto Vondelstraat, and enter the park about a block down. The Institute is on the left. ⓢ Screenings €8, students and with Museumjaarkaart €6.70. 🕑 Open M-F 9am-10pm, Sa-Su from 1hr. before the 1st show to 10:15pm. Library open M-Tu 1-5pm, Th-F 1-5pm.

🎦 Pathe Tuschinski
REMBRANDTPLEIN

Reguliersbreestraat 26-28

☎020 626 26 33; www.tuschinski.nl

One of Europe's first experiments with Art Deco design, this 1921 theater maintains its original luxury, but now boasts better technology. Watch new Hollywood releases from the comfort of some of the biggest, cushiest seats you'll ever sit in. Catch artsier fare at the **Tuschinski Arthouse** next door.

▶ 🚋 Tram #9 or 14 to Rembrandtplein. Walk down Reguliersbreestraat, and you'll see the cinema on the right. ⓢ Tickets €7.80-10. ⓘ Open daily from 11:30am.

SAUNAS AND SPAS

Saunas and spas fall into two categories: those intended for indulgent pampering, and gay saunas where people go to indulge in the other pleasures of the flesh. It should be fairly obvious which are which, but, if you want to be sure, a quick Google search never hurt anyone.

Sauna Deco
CANAL RING WEST

Herengracht 115

☎020 623 82 15; www.saunadeco.nl

Inside a stunning Art Deco interior (with ornaments from the original Le Bon Marché store on rue de Sèvres in Paris), bathers enjoy a sauna, steam room, plunge bath, and spa offering services from massages to facials. The patio garden and lounge beds make it the perfect place to relax even on dry land. All bathing is unisex.

▶ 🚋 Tram #1, 2, 5, 14, or 17 to Nieuwezijds Kolk. Walk east, cross the Singel, and turn left onto Herengracht. ⓢ Sauna €21. Towel rental €2. 25min. massage €30, 55min. €55. Cash only. ⓘ Open M noon-11pm, Tu 3-11pm, W-Sa noon-11pm, Su 1-7pm.

Thermos
LEIDSEPLEIN

Raamstraat 33

☎020 623 91 58; www.thermos.nl

Thermos is one of the oldest and largest gay saunas in Europe. Its day and night branches were recently fused together into one complex, making it possible to stay from lunchtime till breakfast the next day (although you'd likely get pretty pruney). It has a Finnish sauna, Turkish steam bath, whirlpool, swimming pool, video room, private rooms, beauty salon, bar, and restaurant.

Depending on the season, there may be a lot of tourists, but Thermos generally attracts a slightly older clientele.

▶ 🚋 Tram #7 or 10 to Raamplein. *i* 16+. Men only. ⓢ €19.50, under 25 and over 65 €10. ⓓ Open daily noon-8am.

COFFEESHOPS

Once upon a time, Amsterdam allowed tourists from far and wide to flock to its canals for cheap, legal drugs at its famous "coffeeshops." But those days have come and gone, and, as of late 2011, Dutch officials were planning to limit the use of legal marijuana to Dutch citizens. New regulations aside, coffeeshops and the relative permissability of soft drugs in the Netherlands provide a fascinating window into Dutch culture and society. The listings that follow represent but a small introduction to the vast world of Amsterdam coffeeshops. If you happen to be Dutch, or if the government suddenly backtracks, you'll be able to get into them. The exact impact of the new regulations is hard to predict at the time of publishing, so we encourage you to do some research if you're interested in learning more about coffeeshops. Finally, though we may list a number of coffeeshops, *Let's Go* does not recommend drug use in any form.

📕 Paradox   JORDAAN
1e Bloemdwarsstraat 2
☎020 623 56 39; www.paradoxcoffeeshop.com

Come to this local gem for the product, and stay for the chill atmosphere. The walls and furniture are covered in oddball art (one table is adorned with a painting of a bare-breasted, two-headed mermaid), while bongs, vaporizers, and bowls are on hand. Select from over a dozen types of weed and an usually broad selection of joints. A helpful menu describes the effects of each variety, making it easy to get exactly what you want. If you're still confused, the staff is happy to help.

▶ 🚋 Tram #13, 14, or 17 to Westermarkt. Cross Prinsengracht and continue on Rozengracht, then make a left onto 1e Bloemdwarsstraat. ⓢ Joints €3-5; weed €5.50-11 per g; hash €7-15 per g; space cakes €6. ⓓ Open daily 10am-8pm.

📕 Amnesia   CANAL RING WEST
Herengracht 133
☎020 427 78 74

Amnesia is a well-regarded coffeeshop with a gorgeous canal view

> ### Move Over, Mushrooms
>
> Holland may have a reputation as the land where "anything goes," but every country has its limits. In December 2008, in an effort to save face internationally, the government outlawed magic mushrooms. Dutch smartshops have lived up to their name, out-smarting the ban by turning instead to truffles. Also known as Philosopher's Stones, truffles can be eaten raw like mushrooms, and, because they contain the same hallucinogenic compounds (psilocin and psilocybin), they have a similar psychoactive effect. Some truffles might make you laugh, while others will give you a more mystical or contemplative high, and some will have you seeing brightly colored kaleidoscopic patterns everywhere you look. *Let's Go* never recommends drug use, but if you are considering trying truffles, talk to the people at the smartshop about the safest way to experience them.

and high-quality products, highlighted by nine Cannabis Cup winners. There's also a large coffee bar for those who prefer the stimulating effects of caffeine to those of the other drugs on offer.

▶ Tram #1, 2, 5, 13, 14, or 17 to Dam/Radhuisstraat. Continue along Radhuisstraat and turn right onto Herengracht. ⓢ Joints €4-6; weed €8.50-13 per g; specialty brands €13-17 per g. ⓩ Open daily 10am-1am.

Azarius   CENTRAL CANAL RING
Kerkstraat 119
☎020 489 79 14; www.azarius.net

The best thing about this smartshop (a shop that sells psychoactive drugs rather than marijuana) is its knowledgeable staff, who are eager to answer any questions about their products. They sell magic truffles, salvia, herbal XTC, and other herbs and extracts as well as cannabis seeds and various smoking paraphernalia. If you can't find what you're looking for, Azarius also runs the world's largest online smartshop.

▶ Tram #1, 2, or 5 to Prinsengracht. Walk 1 block up Leidsestraat and make a right onto Kerkstraat. ⓢ Truffles €10-14. ⓩ Open in summer daily noon-9pm; fall-spring M-Tu noon-9pm, Th-Sa noon-9pm.

De Tweede Kamer   NIEUWE ZIJD
Heisteeg 6
☎020 422 22 36

It looks like a regular Dutch *bruin cafe,* but don't be fooled—De

Tweede Kamer has one of the most extensive menus of any coffeeshop in Amsterdam, categorized by type, smell, flavor, and quality of the high. Plus, there's something fun about smoking in a store named after one of the Dutch chambers of Parliament.

▶ 🚋 Tram #1, 2, or 5 to Spui/Nieuwezijds Voorburgwal. Walk down to Spui, up Spuistraat, and turn left onto Heisteeg. ⑤ Joints €3-9; weed €4-13 per g; hash €8-40 per g; space cakes and muffins €6. ⏰ Open daily 10am-1am.

Tweedy
MUSEUMPLEIN AND VONDELPARK

2e Constantijn Huygensstraat 76
☎020 618 03 44

Tweedy is located just a short walk from a classy museum (the Van Gogh Museum), a beautiful park (Vondelpark), and a repurposed squat (OT301). Hit all of them plus this coffeeshop in one day, and you'll have seen just about everything that matters in Amsterdam. Tweedy's selection is small but cheap and includes quality favorites like White Widow. A steady stream of reggae will join you in the relaxing basement-like smoking area.

▶ 🚋 Tram #1 to 1e Con. Huygensstraat or tram #3 or 12 to Overtoom. Walk down Overtoom and make a left onto 2e Con. Huygensstraat. ⑤ Joints €3.50; weed €5-11 per g; hash €6-10 per g. ⏰ Open daily 11am-11pm.

The Bush Doctor
REMBRANDTPLEIN

Thorbeckeplein 28
☎020 330 74 75

This small store boasts two floors and outdoor seating that spills out onto Thorbeckeplein. The drug menu caters to the serious and experienced smoker, making it one of the best places to try specialty strains of weed and hash. Not only does the Bush Doctor have a variety of their own potent mixes, various fruity options, and organic wares, but they also carry half a dozen kinds of the infamous ice-o-lator hash. The best part of this shop is its location, just a short distance away from Studio 80 and the other clubs of Rembrandtplein, and not too far from the bars in Leidseplein.

▶ 🚋 Tram #9 or 14 to Rembrandtplein. Thorbeckeplein is across the square from the giant TV screen. ⑤ Joints €4-6; weed €7.50-12.50 per g; hash €10-12 per g, ice-o-lator €22-55 per g; space cakes €7. ⏰ Open daily 9am-1am.

Shopping

With shopping, as with pretty much everything else, Amsterdam accommodates both snooty European intellectuals and renegade rasta men. The Nine Streets just south of Westerkerk are packed with vintage stores and interesting boutiques. Haarlemmerstraat, in Scheepvaartbuurt, is an up-and-coming design district. For more established brands, look to Kalverstraat, with its string of international chains and large department stores. For something really pricey, P. C. Hooftstraat, near Museumplein, is home to all the big-name designers. On the other end of the spectrum, markets like Albert Cuypmarkt and Waterlooplein offer dirt-cheap and, at times, flat-out bizarre clothing and other miscellaneous wares.

Budget Shopping

Amsterdam is a quirky city. You will find vendors charging extravagant prices for junk that looks like it was just pulled out of the garbage, as well as merchants selling quality second-hand merchandise for dirt cheap. As much as we love living alternatively, rip your own jeans and save money. For a one-stop-cures-all shopping excursion that won't cost you much, head to De Pijp to see the original supermarket, Albert Cuypmarkt. For basic, CVS-like needs, check out the other Albert—Albert Heijn.

CLOTHING AND JEWELRY

SPRMRKT   JORDAAN
Rozengracht 191-193
☎020 330 56 01; www.sprmrkt.nl

Too cool for school (or for vowels, at least), this large store in the Jordaan sells excruciatingly hip streetwear for men and women. The store-within-the-store, SPR+, sells even nicer designer pieces.

▶ 🚋 Tram #10, 13, 14, or 17 to Rozengracht/Marnixstraat. Walk a few blocks down Rozengracht; the store is on the right. ⓘ Open Tu-W 10am-6pm, Th 10am-8pm, F-Sa 10am-6pm, Su noon-6pm.

Studio 88   DE PIJP
Gerard Douplein 88
☎020 770 65 84; www.fashionstudio88.nl

Sometimes it feels like affordable Albert Cuypmarkt isn't a deal, because you won't even wear the clothes. The items at Studio 88 might not have the same rock-bottom prices, but the overstock and sample attire let you get high-end pieces for a fraction of the original cost. The store mostly carries women's clothes, with a few racks of men's things in the back and a small selection of kid's attire.

▶ 🚋 Tram #16 or 24 to Albert Cuypstraat. Walk 1 block up (toward the canal) and turn right onto Gerard Doustraat. The store is up 2 blocks on the right. ⓢ Shirts around €20. Dresses around €40. ⓘ Open M 1-6pm, Tu-F 11am-6pm, Sa 10am-6pm.

Vezjun   JORDAAN
Rozengracht 110
www.vezjun.nl

Vezjun is a small store that specializes in clothing from young, independent Dutch designers. The clothes are occasionally a little out there, but they are well constructed, fresh, and modern. You can be sure no one else will be wearing the same thing at the next party—but you'll be paying for that peace of mind.

▶ 🚋 Tram #10, 13, 14, or 17 to Rozengracht/Marnixstraat. Walk a few blocks east on Rozengracht; the store is on the left. ⓢ Dresses €70-90. ⓘ Open Tu-F noon-7pm, Sa 11am-6pm.

BOOKS

🔖 The Book Exchange
OUDE ZIJD

Kloveniersburgwal 58

☎020 626 62 66; www.bookexchange.nl

The Book Exchange stocks a tremendous inventory of secondhand books, ranging from New Age philosophy to poetry. They have a particularly large selection of paperback fiction. The knowledgeable expat owner is more than happy to chat at length with customers. As the name suggests, the shop also buys and trades books.

▶ 🚋 From Nieuwmarkt, cross to the far side of Kloveniersburgwal and make a left. 🕐 Open M-Sa 10am-6pm, Su 11:30am-4pm.

American Book Center
NIEUWE ZIJD

Spui 2

☎020 625 55 37; www.abc.nl

A centrally located English-language bookstore with a wide range of new and classic titles, American Book Center also has an excellent selection of maps of Amsterdam, from the simple to the more-detailed-than-you-could-ever-have-need-for.

▶ 🚋 Tram #1, 2, or 5 to Spui/Nieuwezijds Voorburgwal. It's on the northern edge of the square. *i* 10% discount for students and teachers with ID. 🕐 Open M 11am-8pm, Tu-W 10am-8pm, Th 10am-9pm, F-Sa 10am-8pm, Su 11am-6:30pm.

The English Bookshop
JORDAAN

Lauriergracht 71

☎020 626 42 30; www.englishbookshop.nl

This small, cozy shop in the Jordaan draws a vibrant community of regulars who enjoy coffee, tea, and fresh pastries while browsing the wide selection of English-language books. The store hosts events like writing workshops, a monthly book club, and the quirky 🔖**literary Trivial Pursuit.**

▶ 🚋 Tram #10, 13, 14, or 17 to Rozengracht/Marnixstraat. Cross Lijnbaansgracht, make a right, and then a left onto Lauriergracht. 🕐 Open Tu-Sa 11am-6pm.

ANTIQUES AND VINTAGE CLOTHING

The **Nine Streets** area in Canal Ring West is the place to find quirky stores selling antiques and vintage swag. For slightly cheaper options, check out the smaller stores on **Haarlemmerstraat.**

Laura Dols
CANAL RING WEST
Wolvenstraat 7
☎020 624 90 66; www.lauradols.nl

Laura Dols specializes in vintage gowns, including taffeta prom dresses, fluffy shepherdess numbers, and things you could actually get away with wearing outside of the house. It also sells shoes, bags, and old-school lingerie (including some awesome metallic bras).

▶ ⚡ Tram #1, 2, or 5 to Spui/Nieuwezijds Voorburgwal. Walk west to the far side of Herengracht, make a right, and then turn left onto Wolvenstraat. ⓢ Most dresses €30-60. ⓘ Open M-W 11am-6pm, Th 11am-9pm, F-Sa 11am-6pm, Su 1-6pm.

Petticoat
JORDAAN
Lindengracht 99
☎020 623 30 65

Come to Petticoat for a good selection of secondhand men's and women's clothing, some from fairly upscale brands. It's unusual to find such an affordable option in the Jordaan, or anywhere in the city for that matter.

▶ ⚡ Tram #3 to Nieuwe Willemstraat. Cross Lijnbaansgracht, make a right, and then turn left onto Lindengracht. ⓢ Tops from €10. Bottoms from €15. ⓘ Open M 11am-6pm, W-F 11am-6pm, Sa 11am-5pm.

Lady Day
CANAL RING WEST
Hartenstraat 9
☎020 623 58 20; www.theninestreets.com/ladyday

An established go-to spot for '50s, '60s, and '70s vintage style, Lady Day offers a massive collection of men's and women's clothes: tweed jackets, cocktail dresses, bathing suits, sweaters, tops, scarves, and much more. Most of the clothes are still quite fashionable, and the things that aren't are still really cheap.

▶ ⚡ Tram #13, 14, or 17 to Westermarkt. Walk down Radhuisstraat to the far side of Keizersgracht, make a right, and then turn left onto Hartenstraat. ⓢ Dresses around €25. Sweaters €20. Scarves €1. ⓘ Open M-W 11am-6pm, Th 11am-9pm, F-Sa 11am-6pm, Su 1-6pm.

MARKETS

Albert Cuypmarkt
DE PIJP
Albert Cuypstraat

Stretching almost half a mile along the length of Albert

Cuypstraat, this is the most famous market in the city. Need a motorcycle helmet, sundress, and cinnamon all in one afternoon? Albert Cuypmarkt is the place to go. The clothes can be hit-or-miss, but for produce or knick-knacks, it's a great option. Rows of stores behind the market stalls sell similar items at slightly higher prices (though the clothes are a bit more wearable). Be sure to come early if you want to see the full display—some vendors start packing up as early as 4pm.

▶ Tram #16 or 24 to Albert Cuypstraat. Open M-Sa 9am-6pm.

Noordermarkt

JORDAAN

Noordermarkt
www.boerenmarktamsterdam.nl

This organic market pops up every Saturday in a picturesque northern corner of the Jordaan to sell produce, cheese, baked goods, herbs, homeopathic remedies, and some hippie-esque clothes. Noordermarkt is a great place to shop or browse when you can't afford the Jordaan's classy indoor boutiques.

▶ Tram #3 to Nieuwe Willemstraat. Cross Lijnbaansgracht, walk up Willemstraat, make a right onto Brouwersgracht, and then another right onto Prinsengracht. The market is about a block down. Open Sa 9am-4pm.

Dappermarkt

OUTSKIRTS

Dapperstraat
www.dappermarkt.nl

Dappermarkt exudes the vibrant local flavor of Amsterdam East, blending the city's old charm with the cultures of its North African and Middle Eastern immigrant communities. Come here to find vegetables, spices, cloth, furniture, clothes, and more at cheaper prices than the touristy markets in the city center. It's near Oosterpark, just south of Plantage.

▶ Tram #3 or 7 to Dapperstraat. Walk south on Wijttenbachstraat and make the 1st right onto Dapperstraat. Open M-Sa 9am-5pm.

SMOKING ACCESSORIES AND MUSIC

Smartshops and larger coffeeshops often have wide selections of drug toys, from pipes to bongs to one-hitters in all colors, shapes, and sizes. Amsterdam also has some excellent music stores and quirky secondhand music can be found at some of the markets.

Got Wood?

Wooden shoes may sound bizarre, but this is Amsterdam, so obviously that isn't stopping them. The traditional shoes can be traced back to the Germanic tribes who were the original occupants of the Netherlands. Over a century ago, they were used to protect the feet of factory workers, miners, and farmers. Known as *klompen*, these clogs can withstand almost anything that would threaten a worker's feet with harm, including sharp objects and acid.

You're not likely to find a native strolling the city in this old-fashioned style, but they are still a common (and cliché) souvenir among tourists. And some people do indeed wear them while working in the garden or on the farm. Have a green thumb yourself? Take a pair home, and garden like the Dutch.

Concerto
CENTRAL CANAL RING

Utrechtsestraat 52-60

☎020 623 52 28; www.platomania.eu

Multiple storefronts make up this huge complex with the biggest music selection in Amsterdam. Concerto sells records, DVDs, and secondhand CDs in almost every genre imaginable. It's also a great place to check out flyers and posters for upcoming concerts and festivals. You can even purchase some show tickets here.

▶ ✈ Tram #4, 7, 10, or 25 to Fredericksplein. Walk diagonally across the square and up Utrechtsestraat. ⌚ Open M-W 10am-6pm, Th 10am-9pm, F-Sa 10am-6pm, Su noon-6pm.

South Miami Plaza
DE PIJP

Albert Cuypstraat 116

☎020 662 28 17; www.southmiamiplaza.nl

Come here for a fine selection of pop, blues, reggae, R and B, world music, and a special section of Dutch classics (trust us, browsing the covers alone is a worthwhile endeavor). They also have plenty of DVDs. Bargain bins hold an eclectic mix of CDs that start at just €1.

▶ ✈ Tram #16 or 24 to Albert Cuypstraat. Walk through the market and the store is on the right. ⌚ Open M-Sa 10am-6pm.

The Old Man
NIEUWE ZIJD

Damstraat 16

☎020 627 00 43; www.theoldman.com

This large store near Dam Sq. sells smoking accessories, boardsport equipment, and knives—we just hope no one uses all three at once. Paraphernalia ranges from tiny pipes to bongs to grinders. The Old Man's products aren't necessarily better than what you'd find at a smartshop, but there's a wider variety and quirkier options. Case in point: the bong in the shape of a clog—clearly the Dutch souvenir your grandmother is hoping for.

▶ 🚋 1 of the many trams to Dam. Walk to the end of the square and make a left. 🕒 Open M-W 10am-6pm, Th-F 10am-9pm, Sa-Su 10am-6pm.

Velvet Music
JORDAAN

Rozengracht 40

☎020 422 87 77; www.velvetmusic.nl

Velvet carries the latest releases and older music in virtually every genre, with an especially good selection of the diverse kinds of sounds that get lumped together as "indie". Smaller than Concerto, but less overwhelming to navigate, the shop also buys used music and has a large selection of vinyl.

▶ 🚋 Tram #13, 14, or 17 to Westermarkt. Cross Prinsengracht and walk down Rozengracht. 🕒 Open M noon-6pm, Tu-Sa 10am-6pm.

Essentials

You don't have to be a rocket scientist to plan a good trip. (It might help, but it's not required.) You do, however, need to be well prepared, and that's what we can do for you. Essentials is the chapter that gives you all the nitty-gritty you need to know for your trip: the hard information gleaned from 50 years of collective wisdom and several months of furious fact-checking. Planning your trip? Check. Where to find Wi-Fi? Check. The dirt on public transportation? Check. We've also thrown in communications info, safety tips, and a phrasebook, just for good measure. Plus, for overall trip-planning advice from what to pack (money and as little underwear as possible) to how to take a good passport photo (it's physically impossible; consider airbrushing), you can also check out the Essentials section of www.letsgo.com.

So, flick through this chapter before you leave so you know what documents to bring, while you're on the plane so you know how you'll be getting from the airport to your accommodation, and when you're on the ground so you can find a laundromat to solve all your 3am stain-removal needs. This chapter may not always be the most scintillating read, but it just might save your life.

RED TAPE

Documents and Formalities

We're going to fill you in on visas and work permits, but don't forget the most important one of all: your passport. **Don't forget your passport!**

Visas

EU citizens don't need a visa to visit the The Netherlands. Citizens of Australia, Canada, New Zealand, the US, and other non-EU countries do not need a visa for stays of up to 90 days, but this three-month period begins upon entry into any of the countries that belong to the EU's **freedom of movement** zone. For more information, see **One Europe** (below). Those staying longer than 90 days may apply for a longer-term visa; consult an embassy or consulate for more information.

Though a visa isn't necessary for EU citizens, Dutch officials are known to be universal sticklers about visas and reasons for travel. Most questions consist of just the regular "Why are you here? How long are you staying?" That being said, make sure your reasons for travel are legitimate and that you can give an approximate length for your visit.

Work Permits

Admittance to The Netherlands as a traveler does not include the right to work, which is authorized only by a work permit. For more information, see the **Beyond Tourism** chapter.

Embassies and Consulates

- **DUTCH CONSULAR SERVICES IN AUSTRALIA: Consulate General.** (Level 26, Westfield Tower 2, 101 Grafton St., Bondi Junction NSW, 2022 ☎020 9387 6644; www.netherlands.org.au ✆ Open M-F 10am-1pm.)

- **DUTCH CONSULAR SERVICES IN CANADA: Consulate General.** (1 Dundas St. W, Ste. 2106, Toronto, ON M5G 1Z3

☎877-388-2443; http://ottawa.the-netherlands.org ⏰ Open M-F 9am-noon.)

- **DUTCH CONSULAR SERVICES IN IRELAND: Embassy.** (160 Merrion Rd., Dublin 4 ☎01 269 3444; http://ireland.nlembassy.org ⏰ Open M-F 9am-11:30pm.)

- **DUTCH CONSULAR SERVICES IN NEW ZEALAND: Embassy.** (PSIS House, 10th fl., Wellington ☎04 471 6390; www.netherlandsembassy.co.nz ⏰ Open M-Th 8:30am-5pm, F 8:30am-2pm.)

- **DUTCH CONSULAR SERVICES IN THE UNITED KINGDOM. Embassy.** (38 Hyde Park Gate, London, SW7 5DP ☎020 7590 3200; www.dutchembassyuk.org *i* Appointments required; schedule one online. ⏰ Open M-F 8:30am-noon, closed 1st and 3rd W each month.)

- **DUTCH CONSULAR SERVICES IN THE USA: Embassy.** (4200 Linnean Ave. NW, Washington, DC, 20008 ☎877-388-2443; http://dc.the-netherlands.org *i* Appointments required; schedule one online. ⏰ Open M-F 9am-4:30pm.)

Embassies in the Netherlands are situated in The Hague, but the UK and the US have Consulate Generals in Amsterdam.

- **AUSTRALIAN CONSULAR SERVICES IN THE NETHERLANDS: Embassy.** (Carnegielaan 4, 2517 KH, The Hague ☎070 310 82 00; www.netherlands.embassy.gov.au ⏰ Open M-F 8:30am-5pm.)

- **CANADIAN CONSULAR SERVICES IN THE NETHERLANDS: Embassy.** (Sophialaan 7, 2514 JP, The Hague ☎070 311 16 00; www.canada.nl ⏰ Open May 16-Sept 2 M-Th 8:30am-12:30pm and 1:15-5:30pm, F 8:30am-1pm; Sept 5-May 14 M-F 9am-1pm and 2-5:30pm.)

- **IRISH CONSULAR SERVICES IN THE NETHERLANDS: Embassy.** (Scheveningseweg 112, 2584 AE, The Hague ☎070 363 09 93; www.irishembassy.nl ⏰ Open M-F 10am-12:30pm and 2:30-5pm.)

- **NEW ZEALAND CONSULAR SERVICES IN THE NETHERLANDS: Embassy.** (Eisenhowerlaan 77N, 2517 KK, The

Hague ☎070 346 93 24; www.nzembassy.com/netherlands 🕐 Open M-F 9am-12:30pm and 1:30-5pm.)

- **BRITISH CONSULAR SERVICES IN THE NETHERLANDS: Consulate General.** (Koningslaan 44 ☎020 676 43 43; http://ukinnl.fco.gov.uk 🕐 Open M-Tu 9am-1pm, Th-F 9am-1pm.)

- **AMERICAN CONSULAR SERVICES IN THE NETHERLANDS: Consulate General.** (Museumplein 19 ☎020 575 53 09; http://amsterdam.usconsulate.gov *i* All non-emergency visits require online appointment. 🕐 Open for emergency visits M-F 8:30-11:30am.)

PRACTICALITIES

For all the hostels, cafes, museums, and bars we list, we know some of the most important places you visit during your trip might actually be more mundane. Whether it's a tourist office, internet cafe, or post office, these practicalities are vital to a successful trip, and you'll find all you need right here.

- **TOURIST OFFICES: VVV** provides information on sights, museums, performances, and accommodations. They also sell the **I Amsterdam** card, which gives you unlimited transport and free admission to many museums for a set number of days. For other transportation information, you're better off going to the **GVB office** next door. The lines at the office by Centraal Station can be unbearably long, so unless you need information right after you step off the train, try the one in Leidseplein instead. (Stationsplein 10 ☎020 201 88 00; www.iamsterdam.com ✱ Across from the eastern part of Centraal Station, near tram stops #1-4. 🕐 Open July-Aug daily 9am-7pm; Sept-June M-Sa 9am-6pm, Su 9am-5pm.) Other locations at **Schiphol Airport** (Aankomstpassage 40, in Arrival Hall 2 🕐 Open daily 7am-10pm.) and **Leidseplein 26.** (🕐 Open M-F 10am-7:30pm, Sa 10am-6pm, Su noon-6pm.)

- **GLBT RESOURCES: GAYtic** is a tourist office that specializes in GLBT info, and is authorized by the VVV. (Spuistraat 4 ☎020 330 14 61; www.gaytic.nl ✱ Tram #1, 2, 5, 13, or 17 to Nieuwezijds Kolk. Walk 1 block west to Spuistraat; the office is inside the Gays and Gadgets store. ☏ Open M-Sa 11am-8pm, Su noon-8pm.) **Pink Point** provides information on GLBT issues, events, and attractions in the city, and sells all kinds of GLBT souvenirs. (Westermarkt, by the Homomonument ☏020 428 10 70; www.pinkpoint.org ✈ Tram #13, 14, or 17 to Westermarkt. ☏ Open daily 10am-6pm; reduced hours in winter.) **Gay and Lesbian Switchboard** provides anonymous assistance for any GLBT-related questions or concerns. (☏020 623 65 65; www.switchboard.nl ☏ Operates M-F 2-6pm.)

- **LAUNDROMATS: Rozengracht Wasserette** sells detergent and provides self-service and next-day laundry. (Rozengracht 59 ☏020 063 59 75 ✈ Tram #13, 14, or 17 to Westermarkt. Cross Prinsengracht and walk a few blocks down Rozengracht. ⓢ Wash €8, dry €7. ☏ Open daily 9am-9pm.) **Powders Launderette.** (Kerkstraat 56 ☏062 630 60 57; www.powders.nl ✈ Tram #1, 2, 5, 7, or 10 to Leidseplein. Walk up Leidsestraat and make a right. *i* Detergent for sale. Wi-Fi. ⓢ Wash €4.50 per hr.; dry €0.50 per 11min. 5kg wash, dry, and fold €10. ☏ Self-service open daily 7am-10pm. Full-service open M-W 8am-5pm, F 8am-5pm, Sa-Su 9am-3pm.)

- **INTERNET: Openbare Bibliotheek Amsterdam** provides free Wi-Fi and free use of computers that can be reserved through the information desk. (Oosterdokskade 143 ☏020 523 09 00; www.oba.nl ✈ From Centraal Station, walk east, sticking close to the station building. You'll cross a canal, and the street will become Oosterdokskade. ☏ Open daily 10am-10pm.) **The Mad Processor** is popular with gamers. (Kinkerstraat 11-13 ☏020 612 18 18; www.madprocessor.nl ✈ Tram #7, 10, or 17 to Elandsgracht. Cross Nassaukade onto Kinkerstraat. *i* Computers with Skype. Fax machines and scanners available. ⓢ Internet €1 per 30min. Printing €0.20 per page. ☏ Open daily noon-2am.)

- **POST OFFICES:** The main branch can deal with all of your postal needs, plus it has banking services and sells phone cards. (Singel 250 ☏020 556 33 11; www.tntpost.nl ✈ Tram #1, 2, 5, 13, 14, or 17 to Dam. Walk on Raadhuisstraat away from the square and make a left onto Singel. The post office is in the basement. ☏ Open M-F 7:30am-6:30pm, Sa 7:30am-5pm.) You can also buy stamps and send packages from any store that has the orange and white TNT sign (including many grocery stores and tobacco shops).

- **POSTAL CODES:** Range from 1000 AA to 1099 ZZ. Check http://maps.google.nl or www.tntpost.com to find out the code for a specific address.

Emergency

Practicalities are great, but some things are particularly important, and we present those to you here. Hopefully you never need any of these things, but if you do, it's best to be prepared.

- **EMERGENCY NUMBER:** ☎112.

- **POLICE: Politie Amsterdam-Amstelland** is the Amsterdam police department. Dialing ☎0900 8844 will connect you to the nearest station or rape crisis center. The following stations are located in and around the city center. **Lijnbaansgracht.** (Lijnbaansgracht 219 ☏ Tram #7 or 10 to Raamplein. Walk 1 block south and make a left onto Leidsegracht. ⌚ Open 24hr.) **Nieuwezijds Voorburgwal.** (Nieuwezijds Voorburgwal 104-108 ☏ Tram #1, 2, 5, 13, or 17 to Nieuwezijds Kolk. Walk 1 block down Nieuwezijds Voorburgwal, away from Centraal Station. ⌚ Open 24hr.) **Prinsengracht.** (Prinsengracht 1109 ☏ Tram #4, 7, 10, or 25 to Frederiksplein. Walk north diagonally through the square, up Utrechtsestraat, and make a right onto Prinsengracht. ⌚ Open 24hr.) From outside the Netherlands, you can call the Amsterdam police at ☎+31 20 559 91 11.

- **CRISIS HOTLINES: Telephone Helpline** provides general counseling services. (☎020 675 75 75 ⌚ Operates 24hr.) **Amsterdam Tourist Assistance Service** provides help for victimized tourists, generally those who have been robbed. They offer assistance with transferring money, replacing documents, and finding temporary accommodations. (Nieuwezijds Voorburgwal 104-08 ☎020 625 32 46; www.stichtingatas.nl ☏ Tram #1, 2, 5, 13, or 17 to Nieuwezijds Kolk. Walk 1 block down Nieuwezijds Voorburgwal. It's inside the police station. ⌚ Open daily 10am-10pm.) **Sexual Abuse Hotline** provides information and assistance to victims of domestic violence, abuse, and rape. (☎020 611 60 22 ⏰ Operates 24hr.)

- **LATE-NIGHT PHARMACIES: Afdeling Inlichtingen Apotheken Hotline** provides information about which pharmacies are open late on a given day. (☎020 694 87 09 ⏰ Operates 24hr.) You can also check posted signs on the doors of closed pharmacies to find the nearest one open in the area. There are no specifically designated 24hr. pharmacies, but there are always a few open at any given time.

- **HOSPITALS/MEDICAL SERVICES: Academisch Meidisch Centrum** is one of two large university hospitals in Amsterdam. Located southeast of the city, past the Amsterdam Arena stadium. (Meibergdreef 9 ☎020 566 91 11; www.amc.uva.nl 🚌 Bus #45, 47, 355 or Metro trains #50 or 54 to Holendrecht. The hospital is directly across. ⏰ Open 24hr.) **Tourist Medical Service** provides doctor's visits for guests at registered hotels and runs a 24hr. line to connect tourists to non-emergency medical care. (☎020 592 33 55; www.tmsdoctor.nl ⏰ Operates 24hr.)

GETTING THERE

By Plane

Schiphol Airport (AMS) is the main international airport for the Netherlands. (☎020 900 01 41 from the Netherlands, +31 207 940 800 from elsewhere; www.schiphol.nl) It's located 18km outside the city center. The easiest way to reach Centraal Station from the airport is by train. (💲 €4.20. ⏰ 15-20min.; 4-10 per hr. 6am-1am, 1 per hr. 1am-6am.) The train station is located just below the airport; you can buy tickets at machines with cards or coins, or from the ticket counter with cash. Buses also leave from the airport, which can be useful for travelers who are staying outside the city center. Bus #370 passes by Leidseplein, and other buses travel to Amsterdam and neighboring towns.

By Train

Within the Netherlands, the easiest way to reach Amsterdam is by train, which will almost certainly run to **Centraal Station**

(Stationsplein 1 ☎020 900 92 92; www.ns.nl). Trains arrive from The Hague (⑤ €10.20. ⏲ 1hr., 3-6 per hr. 4:45am-12:45am.), Rotterdam (⑤ €13.40. ⏲ 1hr.; 3-8 per hr. 5:30am-12:45am, 1 per hr. 12:45am-5:30am.), and Utrecht. (⑤ €6.70. ⏲ 30min.; 4 per hr. 6am-midnight, 1 per hr. midnight-6am.) International trains from Belgium and Paris are operated by **Thalys** (www.thalys.com), which runs trains from Brussels (⑤ €29-69. ⏲ 2hr., 1 per hr. 7:50am-8:50pm.) and Paris. (⑤ €35-120. ⏲ 3hr.)

You'll need to shop around for the best deals on trains to Amsterdam from other major European cities. Check **Rail Europe** (www.raileurope.com) to compare prices for most companies. Like Dutch trains, all international trains run to the glorious potpourri of travelers known as Centraal Station. Train tickets range from €100-300 depending on the destination, and rise rapidly as the date of departure approaches.

By Bus

While buses aren't a great way to get around the Netherlands, they can be cheaper for international travel. **Eurolines** (☎020 560 87 88; www.eurolines.com) is the best choice, and runs buses from Brussels (⑤ €25, under 25 €19. ⏲ 3-4½hr., 7-12 per day) and Bruges (⑤ €25, under 25 €19. ⏲ 5hr., 1 per day) to the **Amsterdam Amstel station,** which is connected to the rest of the city by Metro and tram #12.

If you want to travel to Amsterdam by bus from major cities such as London (⑤ €42.), Munich (⑤ €42.), and Paris (⑤ €84.), you will almost definitely have to go through Brussels, Bruges, and the above-mentioned stops on the way. Eurolines often has deals for those who book in advance.

GETTING AROUND

Tram, bus, and Metro lines extend out from Centraal Station, while more trams and buses cross those routes perpendicularly, or circumnavigate the canal rings. Trams are generally the fastest and easiest mode of transport in Amsterdam, serving almost all major points within the city center. The Red Light District and Oude Zijd only have stops on their northern or southern ends. Buses are good if you are heading outside of the center or to more residential parts of the city, though trams extend to some of these as well. The Metro is rarely useful for tourists, as it only goes down the eastern side of the city and has few stops within the center.

Tickets and information can be found at **GVB.** (☎020 460 60 60; www.gvb.nl ✙ On Stationsplein across from the eastern end of Centraal Station next to the VVV tourist office. ⏰ Open M-F 7am-9pm, Sa-Su 10am-6pm.) The lines here can be long, but it's the easiest place to buy transport tickets. The **OV-chipkaart** (www.ov-chipkaart.nl) has replaced the strippenkaart as the only type of ticket used on Amsterdam public transport. Disposable tickets can be purchased when boarding trams and buses. (⑤ 1hr. ticket €2.60, 1- to 7-day tickets €7-30.) A personalized OV-chipkaart, featuring the owner's picture and allowing perks like automatically adding value when the balance is low, is a good option if you're staying in Amsterdam for a long time. You're more likely, however, to get an anonymous card, which can be purchased for €7.50 (plus an extra €5 as a starting balance), and can be reloaded at machines located throughout the city (most visibly in major supermarkets like Albert Heijn).

You must both tap in and tap out with your chipkaart to avoid being charged for more than you actually travel. With the chipkaart, a ride on the bus, tram, or Metro costs €0.79 plus €0.10 per km. Most rides within the city center will cost around €1-2. Most transport runs 5am-midnight; after that, there are 12 night bus lines that run once per hour, twice per hour on weekend nights. An ordinary chipkaart does not work on night buses; you must buy special tickets (€4; 12 for €30) or one of the one- to seven-day passes.

Bike Rentals

🛇 Frederic Rent-a-Bike   SCHEEPVAARTBUURT
Brouwersgracht 78
☎020 624 55 09; www.frederic.nl

In addition to rooms and general wisdom re: all things Amsterdam (see **Accommodations**), come here for bike repairs and rentals.

▶ ✙ From Centraal Station, cross the canal, make a right on Prins Hendrikkade, cross the Singel, make a left on Singel, and then a right onto Brouwersgracht. *i* Prices include lock and insurance. No deposit required, just a copy of a credit card or passport. ⑤ Bike rentals €10 per day; €16 per 2 days; €40 per week; €100 per month. ⏰ Open daily 9am-5:30pm.

Bike City   JORDAAN
Bloemgracht 68-70
☎020 626 37 21; www.bikecity.nl

Rentals cost a bit more here than at other shops, but they are well worth it, because the bikes come free from the plastered advertisements attached to most rented bikes in the city. You may even be able to blend in as a local with one of Bike City's plain black rides.

▶ 🚊 Tram #13, 14, or 17 to Westermarkt. Cross Prinsengracht, make a right, and then a left onto Bloemgracht. *i* ID and deposit of a credit card or €50 required. Ⓢ Bike rentals from €10 per 4hr.; €13.50 per 24hr.; up to €43.50 per 5 days. Insurance €2.50 per day. ⏰ Open daily 9am-6pm.

Damstraat Rent-a-Bike   RED LIGHT DISTRICT
Damstraat 22
☎020 625 50 29; www.bikes.nl

Damstraat rents multiple kinds of bikes, including tandems, and also sells new and secondhand bikes.

▶ 🚊 1 of the many trams to Dam. Walk to the end of the square and make a left onto Damstraat. *i* Copy of credit card or ID and €25 deposit required. Ⓢ From €6.50 per 3hr.; €9.50 per 24hr.; €31 per 6 days. Sells bikes from €160. ⏰ Open daily 9am-6pm.

MONEY

Getting Money from Home

Stuff happens, and when it does, you usually need some money. The easiest and cheapest solution is to have someone back home make a deposit to your bank account, but you may also want to consider one of these other options.

Wiring Money

Arranging a **bank money transfer** means asking a bank back home to wire money to a bank in Amsterdam. This is the cheapest way to transfer cash, but it's also the slowest, usually taking several days or more. Note that some banks may only release your funds in local currency, potentially sticking you with a poor exchange rate; inquire about this in advance. The banking system in Amsterdam is modern and well-organized, so you shouldn't run into too much trouble getting yo' dolla-dolla billz from the bank.

Money transfer services like **Western Union** are faster and more convenient than bank transfers—but also much pricier. To find the nearest Western Union location visit www.westernunion.com or call the appropriate number: in Australia ☎1800 173 833, in Canada 800-235-0000, in the UK 0808 234 9168, in the US

800-325-6000, and in The Netherlands 0800 023 5172. Money transfer services are also available to **American Express** cardholders and at selected **Thomas Cook** offices.

US State Department

In case of a serious emergency, the US State Department will help American citizens arrange a wire transfer directly from your family or friends to the nearest consular office, which will then disburse it according to instructions for a US$30 fee. If you wish to use this service, you must contact the Overseas Citizens Services division of the US State Department. (☎+1-202-501-4444, from US 888-407-4747)

Withdrawing Money

To use a debit or credit card to withdraw money from a cash machine (ATM, or *geldautomaat* in Dutch) in Europe, you must have a four-digit Personal Identification Number (PIN). If your PIN is longer than four digits, ask your bank whether you are you able to just use the first four or if you need a new one. Credit cards don't usually come with PINs, so make sure you request one before leaving if you intend to use ATMs while you're abroad.

Where they are accepted, credit cards often offer superior exchange rates—up to 5% better than the retail rate used by banks and other currency exchange establishments. Credit cards may offer services such as insurance and emergency help, and are sometimes required to reserve hotel rooms and rental cars. Unfortunately, less places than you would think accept credit cards in Amsterdam, so check before you order that post-coffeeshop 10-course meal.

Exchange offices in airports and tourist centers usually have unfavorable exchange rates, so go to banks if you need to change your cash into euros.

Tipping

In the Netherlands, service charges are included in the bill at restaurants. This means that waiters do not depend on tips for their livelihood, and you need not fear a proletariat revolution if you choose not to tip. Still, leaving 5-10% for exceptional service is common practice. Tip any higher than that, and you're just showing off. Tipping in bars is rare. For cab drivers, tip around 10%.

Taxes

Advertised prices in the Netherlands include **value added tax (BTW).** This tax on goods is generally levied at 19%, although some goods are subject to a lower rate of 6%.

SAFETY AND HEALTH

General Advice

In any type of crisis, the most important thing to do is **stay calm.** Your country's embassy abroad is usually your best resource in an emergency; registering with your embassy upon arrival in the country is a good idea. The government offices listed in the **Travel Advisories** feature at the end of this section can provide information on the services they offer their citizens in case of emergencies abroad. For a list of helpful hotlines, visit the Access website at (www.access-nl.org).

Local Laws and Police

The Netherlands has some of the most progressive laws in the world, and visitors are often struck by the lack of moral legislation in the country and the efficiency of its legal system. That said, the Netherlands is highly regulated, both by criminal statutes and cultural codes. In the past few years, police have begun to crack down more firmly on illegal activity. If ever in doubt about the limits of Dutch permissiveness, just ask one of the many helpful police officers patrolling Amsterdam's streets.

More popular places like the Red Light District and Leidseplein are often safer places to be late at night than less populated areas like Oud-West. With the prevalence of bicycles in the city, it should come as no surprise that bike theft is one of the biggest crime problems in Amsterdam. If you choose to rent a bike, spend the extra money on a quality bike lock, and always take the time to lock it up well.

Drugs and Alcohol

It hardly needs to be stated that attitudes toward conscience-altering substances are quite different in Amsterdam than other areas of the world, though the city is taking active measures to change this image. The Dutch take a fairly liberal attitude toward alcohol, with the drinking age set at 16 (for alcohol content under 15%—for hard liquor it's 18). Public drunkenness, however, is frowned upon and is a sure way to mark yourself as a tourist.

When it comes to drugs other than alcohol, things get a little more interesting. Whatever anyone standing outside of a club at 4am might tell you, hard drugs are completely illegal, and possession or consumption of substances like heroin and cocaine will be harshly punished. Soft drugs, such as marijuana, are tolerated, but consumption is confined to certain legalized zones, namely coffeeshops (for marijuana) and smartshops (for herbal drugs). Both are heavily regulated but very popular. The number of smartshops in particular has exploded in recent years; however, the use and cultivation of hallucinogenic mushrooms was banned in 2008.

The age of the coffeeshop is also coming to a close. Under new laws passed by the Dutch government, only Dutch residents over the age of 18 will be allowed to enter coffeeshops. As of 2012, customers will have to sign up for a one-year membership, or "dope pass," in order to enter the shops, which have been blamed in recent years for encouraging drug traffficking and encouraging criminal activity. Opponents to the new ban have called it "tourism suicide" and estimate that it will cost the Netherlands millions of tourist euro. Town officials plan on changing old coffeshops into nightclubs or similar nightlife venues. As this book goes to press, the full implications of the laws are unclear, so consult your favorite news source before traveling to learn more about the situation.

Prostitution

The "world's oldest profession" has flourished in the Netherlands, particularly in Amsterdam's famous Red Light District. Legal prostitution comes in two main forms. Window prostitution, which involves scantily clad women tempting passersby from small chambers fronted by a plate-glass window, is by far the most visible. Sex workers of this kind are self-employed and rent the windows themselves. Accordingly, each sets her own price. This form of commercial sex gave the Red Light District its name, as lamps around the windows emit a red glow that, at night, bathes the whole area. Whether shopping or "just looking," be sure to show the women basic respect. Looking is fine and even expected, but leering, catcalling, and other disrespectful behavior are unacceptable. Keep in mind that prostitution is an entirely legal enterprise, and windows are places of business. Most of the prostitutes whom you see belong to a union called "The Red Thread" and are tested for HIV and STIs, although testing is on a voluntary basis. Do not take photos unless you want to explain yourself to the angriest—and largest—man you'll ever see.

If you're interested in having sex with a window prostitute, go up to the door and wait for someone inside to let you in. Show up clean and sober: prostitutes reserve the right to refuse their services. Anything goes as long as you clearly and straightforwardly agree to it beforehand. Specifically state what you want to get for the money you're paying—that means which sex acts, in what positions, and, especially, how much time: by no means are they required to do anything you want without consenting to it in advance. Negotiation occurs and money changes hands before any sexual acts take place.

Always practice safe sex: a prostitute should not and will not touch a penis that is not covered by a condom. Don't ask for a refund if you are left unsatisfied: all sales are final. There is no excuse for making trouble; if anyone becomes violent or threatening with a window prostitute, she has access to an emergency button that sets off a loud alarm. Not only does it make an ear-splitting noise but it also summons the police, who invariably side with prostitutes in disputes. If you feel you have a legitimate complaint or have any questions about commercial sex, head to the extremely helpful Prostitution Information Centre (below).

Another option is the legalized brothels. The term usually refers to an establishment centered on a bar. Women or men will make your acquaintance—and are then available for hour-long sessions. These brothels, also called sex clubs, can be pricey. They are also controversial, and in the past authorities have sought to close brothels associated with trafficking and criminal gangs.

The best place to go for information about prostitution in Amsterdam is the **Prostitution Information Centre.** (Enge Kerksteeg 3, in the Red Light District behind the Oude Kerk, }020 420 7328; www.pic-amsterdam.com ✆ Open Sa 4-7pm. Available at other times for group bookings; call ahead.) Founded in 1994 by Mariska Majoor (once a prostitute herself), the center fills a niche, connecting the Red Light District with its eager visitors.

Specific Concerns

GLBT Travelers

In terms of sexual diversity in Amsterdam, anything goes—and goes often. Darkrooms and dungeons rub elbows with saunas and sex clubs, though much more subdued options are the standard. Many of the patrons at the more explicitly sexual venues are visitors to Amsterdam, not locals. Still, the Netherlands has the most tolerant laws in the world for homosexuals. In 2001, it became the first country to legalize gay marriage, converting all "registered same-sex partnerships" into full marriages. Countless services and establishments cater to GLBT visitors and native Amsterdammers alike.

Nonetheless, certain travelers—including drag queens and kings, other cross-dressers, and transgendered visitors more generally—should take extra caution walking the streets at night, especially around and in the Red Light District. All GLBT visitors to Amsterdam should also be aware that, though the city is a haven of homosexual tolerance, the recent infusion of fundamentalist religiosity into the Dutch political dialogue has created an environment detrimental to complete acceptance of GLBT behaviors and visibility.

Minority Travelers

Despite Amsterdam being known for its openness, there's a lot of hullabaloo about ethnic minorities coming into the Netherlands. Immigrants aren't always welcomed with open arms. Although foreign tourists of all stripes are sometimes treated with suspicion (understandably so, given the regular nuisance they become in the Red Light District), it's mostly non-white visitors who occasionally encounter hostility. Muslims, or those who appear Muslim, seem to run into the most problems. The city is still generally tolerant, but sadly racism is not unheard of.

Pre-Departure Health

Matching a prescription to a foreign equivalent is not always easy, safe, or possible, so if you take **prescription drugs,** carry up-to-date prescriptions or a statement from your doctor stating the medications' trade names, manufacturers, chemical names, and dosages. Be sure to keep all medication with you in your carry-on luggage. It's also a good idea to look up the Dutch names of drugs you may need during your trip.

Immunizations and Precautions

Travelers over two years old should make sure that the following vaccines are up to date: MMR (for measles, mumps, and rubella); DTaP or Td (for diphtheria, tetanus, and pertussis); IPV (for polio); Hib (for *Haemophilus influenzae* B); and HepB (for Hepatitis B). For recommendations on immunizations and prophylaxis, check with a doctor and consult the **Centers for Disease Control and Prevention (CDC)** in the US (☎+1-800-232-4636; www.cdc.gov/travel) or the equivalent in your home country.

Amsterdam is far too cold for mosquitos or animal induced illnesses. The only animal epidemic in Amsterdam is stray cats.

CLIMATE

Amsterdam's weather is mild and temperate, but unpredictable. Like much of Northern Europe, the winters are mostly snowless, but chilly and wet, and the summers are warm and also wet. Because the Netherlands is so flat, winds can bluster from all directions, sweeping away morning clouds or bringing in late-afternoon showers without warning. A combination of the weather and understood classiness results in a conservatively dressed city population. Rainfall is fairly consistent throughout the year, making a raincoat essential attire no matter what time of year you plan to visit. Hot summers do exist, but don't count on it. It's best not to complain about whatever the skies throw your way: nobody comes to Amsterdam for the weather.

MONTH	AVG. HIGH TEMP.		AVG. LOW TEMP.		AVG. RAINFALL		AVG. NUMBER OF WET DAYS
January	5°C	41°F	1°C	34°F	70mm	2.74 in.	17
February	6°C	43°F	0°C	32°F	56mm	2.21 in.	13
March	10°C	50°F	3°C	37°F	67mm	2.63 in.	17
April	14°C	57°F	4°C	39°F	42mm	1.67 in.	14
May	18°C	64°F	8°C	46°F	62mm	2.44 in.	14
June	21°C	70°F	11°C	52°F	66mm	2.58 in.	14
July	23°C	73°F	13°C	55°F	81mm	3.19 in.	13
August	23°C	73°F	13°C	55°F	73mm	2.87 in.	13

September	20°C	68°F	10°C	50°F	78mm 3.08 in.	16
October	16°C	61°F	7°C	45°F	83mm 3.26 in.	17
November	10°C	50°F	3°C	37°F	80mm 3.17 in.	19
December	6°C	43°F	1°C	34°F	76mm 2.98 in.	18

To convert from degrees Fahrenheit to degrees Celsius, subtract 32 and multiply by 5/9. To convert from Celsius to Fahrenheit, multiply by 9/5 and add 32. The mathematically challenged may use this handy chart:

°CELSIUS	-5	0	5	10	15	20	25	30	35	40
°FAHRENHEIT	23	32	41	50	59	68	77	86	95	104

MEASUREMENTS

Like the rest of the rational world, the Netherlands uses the metric system. The basic unit of length is the meter (m), which is divided into 100 centimeters (cm) or 1000 millimeters (mm). One thousand meters make up one kilometer (km). Fluids are measured in liters (L), each divided into 1000 milliliters (mL). A liter of pure water weighs one kilogram (kg), the unit of mass that is divided into 1000 grams (g). One metric ton is 1000kg. It'll probably just be easiest if you check out this chart:

MEASUREMENT CONVERSIONS	
1 inch (in.) = 25.4mm	1 millimeter (mm) = 0.039 in.
1 foot (ft.) = 0.305m	1 meter (m) = 3.28 ft.
1 yard (yd.) = 0.914m	1 meter (m) = 1.094 yd.
1 mile (mi.) = 1.609km	1 kilometer (km) = 0.621 mi.
1 ounce (oz.) = 28.35g	1 gram (g) = 0.035 oz.
1 pound (lb.) = 0.454kg	1 kilogram (kg) = 2.205 lb.
1 fluid ounce (fl. oz.) = 29.57mL	1 milliliter (mL) = 0.034 fl. oz.
1 gallon (gal.) = 3.785L	1 liter (L) = 0.264 gal.

LANGUAGE

Dutch is the official language of the Netherlands, but in Amsterdam most natives speak English—and speak it well. Thanks to mandatory English education in schools and to English-language media exports, most locals have impeccable grammar, vast vocabularies, and a soft continental accent that makes conversing relatively easy. Knowing a few key Dutch words and phrases can't hurt, particularly in smaller towns where English is not spoken as widely. Also, people tend to be more friendly if you at least attempt to speak a little Dutch. Dutch spellings frequently resemble German, but pronunciation is very different. To initiate an English conversation, politely ask, *"Spreekt u Engels?"* (SPRAYKT oo ANG-les?). Even if your conversational counterpart speaks little English, he or she will usually try to communicate, an effort you can acknowledge by thanking them: *"Dank u wel"* (DAHNK oo vell).

Pronunciation

Most Dutch consonants, with a few notable exceptions, share their sounds with their English versions, sometimes rendering Dutch into a phonetic version of English with a foreign accent. Vowels are a different story. The vowels and disphthongs "e," "ee," "i," and "ij" are occasionally pronounced "er" as in "mother." Here are some other counterintuitive pronunciations:

PHONETIC UNIT	PRONUNCIATION	PHONETIC UNIT	PRONUNCIATION
au, ou, or ui	ow, as in "now"	g or ch	kh, as in "loch"
oo	oa, as in "boat"	ie	ee, as in "see"
v	between f and v	j	y, as in "yes"
w	between v and w	ee, ij or ei	ay, as in "layer"
aa	a longer a than in "cat"	oe	oo, as in "shoo"
eu	u, as in "hurt"	uu	a longer oo than in "too"

Phrasebook

ENGLISH	DUTCH	PRONUNCIATION
Hello!/Hi!	Dag!/Hallo!	Dakh!/Hallo!
Goodbye!	Tot ziens!	Tot zeens!
Yes	Ja	Yah
No	Nee	Nay
Sorry!	Sorry!	SOR-ee!
My name is...	Mijn naam is...	Mayn nahm iss...
Do you speak English?	Spreekt u Engels?	Spraykt oo ANG-les?
I don't speak Dutch	Ik spreek geen Nederlands	Ik sprayk khayn NAY-der-lans
I don't understand	Ik begrijp het niet	Ik ber-KHRAYP het neet
Good morning!	Goedemorgen!	KHOO-der-mor-khern!
Good evening!	Goedenavond!	KHOO-der-na-fondt!
Please/You're welcome	Alstublieft	Als-too-BLEEFT
Thank you	Dank u wel	Dahnk oo vell
EMERGENCY		
Go away!	Ga weg!	Kha vekh!
Help!	Help!	Help!

Stop!	Stop!	Stop!
Call the police!	Bel de politie!	Bel der poh-LEET-see!
Get a doctor!	Haal een dokter!	Haal ayn DOK-ter!
I'm sick	Ik ben ziek	Ik ben zeek
I'm lost	Ik ben verdwaald	Ik ben ferd-VAHLDT
QUESTIONS		
Who?	Wie?	Vee?
What?	Wat?	Vat?
When?	Wanneer?	Van-AYR?
Why?	Waarom?	VAR-ohm?
Where is...?	Waar is...?	Vahr iss...?
How do I get to...?	Hoe kom ik in...?	Hoo kom ik in...?
...the museum	...het museum	...het muh-say-um
...the church	...de kerk	...de kerk?
....the bank	...de bank	...de bahnk?
...the hotel	...het hotel	...het ho-TEL
...the shop	...de winkel	...de VIN-kerl
...the market	...de markt	...de markt
...the consulate	...het consulaat	het kon-sul-AAT...
...the train station	...het station	het staht-see-OHN
...the bus stop	...de bushalte	de BUS-hahlter
...the tourist office	...de VVV	de fay fay fay
...the toilet	...het toilet	het tva-LET
What time is it?	Hoe laat is het?	Hoo laht iss het?
Do you have...?	Heeft u...?	Hayft oo...?
How much does this cost?	Wat kost het?	Vat kost het?
ACCOMMODATIONS		
I have a reservation	Ik heb een reservering	Ik hep ayn res-er-VAY-ring
Single room	Eenpersoonskamer	AYN-per-sohn-kah-mer
Double room	Tweepersoonskamer	TVAY-per-sohn-kah-mer
How much per night?	Hoeveel kost per nacht?	Hoo-FAYL kost het per nakht?
FOOD		
We have a reservation	We hebben gereserveerd	Vay HEP-bern kher-ay-ser-VAYRT
Waiter/waitress	Meneer/mevrouw	Mer-NAYR/me-FROW
I'd like...	Ik wil graag...	Ik vil krakh...
May I have the check/bill please?	Mag ik de rekening	Makh ik der Ray-kern-inkh

Amsterdam 101

Amsterdam is celebrated—and demonized—as a center of tolerance for sex, drugs, and rock and roll. Yes, you'll find all of those things, but the Netherlands' legacy is rooted in two more profound pillars: innovation and internationalism. From superiority on the seas to expertise on the easel, the Dutch have blazed a trail through innovative terrain. Credence must be given to the local adage, "God created the world, but the Dutch created the Netherlands." Amsterdammers annexed 3000 square miles of land from the North Sea with an intricate network of ocean-conquering dikes, canals, and pumps. Only a city with this much audacity could pull off Amsterdam's mix of hedonism, world-class art, multicultural sophistication and come-one, come-all openness. Come for the coffeshops; stay for National Windmill Day.

Facts and Figures

- **POPULATION:** 1,360,000
- **SIZE:** 219.4 sq. km
- **CANALS:** 165
- **BRIDGES:** 1281
- **PERCENTAGE OF LAND RESERVED FOR PARKS:** 12%
- **INTERNATIONAL VISITORS ANNUALLY:** 3.7 million
- **COFFEESHOPS IN 1960:** 5
- **COFFEESHOPS TODAY:** 241
- **PERCENTAGE OF DUTCH POPULATION THAT HAS TRIED MARIJUANA:** 20% (compared to 42% of Americans)

HISTORY

Built on Beer (1200-1648)

Amsterdam first took root sometime in the 13th century as a humble fishing village at the mouth of the river Amstel. Inhabitants soon tired of getting their feet wet and decided to build a dam to protect themselves from the river's flooding. Thus was born Amsterdam, "the dam on the Amstel." Amsterdammers eventually realize that switching to the trade business could net them a better income and reduce that awful fish smell. The city got rich quick on the booming beer trade, and became an important site of pilgrimage for Roman Catholics after the so-called **Miracle of Amsterdam**. From what we gather, this involved a dying man puking and something not catching on fire, but you might need to ask a local for the lowdown on why this was so important. The Spanish Empire took over the region in 1506, but the Dutch quickly came to resent the high taxes and religious intolerance imposed by their faraway Catholic overlords. Their ensuing struggle for independence, known as the **80 Years' War,** ended in 1648 when they established the Dutch Republic as a refuge for Europe's religiously persecuted.

Death By Gold (1649-1700)

The 17th century is now known as Amsterdam's **Golden Age.** The Golden Age was marked by loads of trade, some scientific innovation, military expansion, and a Baroque trend in art that infiltrated everything from still lifes to genre paintings. The city's merchants built Amsterdam into the undisputed commercial hub of Northern Europe. The **Dutch East India Company,** the world's first publicly traded multinational corporation, sent ships around the world and established outposts from Japan to South Africa. The city's affluence encouraged a renaissance in art and architecture that gave birth to painters like Rembrandt and Vermeer. While Amsterdam's merchant fleet brought wealth to the city, it also introduced the Bubonic Plague. The epidemic killed 10% of the population from 1663-1666. Amsterdam's mayors, exhibiting all the usefulness we've come to associate with local government, advised inhabitants not to consume salad, spinach, or prunes and recommended tobacco smoke as a protection against the plague.

Growing Pains (1701-1945)

Amsterdam's fabulous wealth encouraged competition, and the Dutch fought a series of wars with rival colonial powers in the 18th century. It turned out the Dutch were much better businessmen than soldiers. They lost many of their overseas colonies to the British and French, and Amsterdam entered a period of economic stagnation and political upheaval. In 1830, Belgium and Luxembourg broke off and the Kingdom of the Netherlands was left substantially smaller.

Amsterdam began to get its mojo back during the Industrial Revolution, but new development led to its own growing pains. New jobs in the city attracted large numbers of peasants from the countryside who soon made up a militant socialist base. Violence between protesters and police became something of a weekly affair.

The Netherlands remained neutral in WWI, though it still suffered from dramatic food shortages. The Dutch didn't get off so easily when WWII hit Europe. The Nazis occupied Amsterdam and shattered Amsterdam's tradition of religious tolerance, sending more than 100,000 Amsterdam Jews to concentration camps. Though many Jews, including **Anne Frank,** went into hiding, the majority did not survive the war, and Amsterdam's formerly robust Jewish community was decimated.

Sex, Drugs, and Rock and Roll (1946-2000)

After a long period of limping recovery after the war, Amsterdam was reborn in the cultural revolution of the 1960s and '70s. The city became known as the *magisch centrum,* or "magical center," of Europe. Soft drugs were legalized, anarchists and squatters laid claim to the streets, and yuppies took over old working-class neighborhoods. This last development marked an important transition in Amsterdam's economy from industry to service and sparked the growth of wealth and finance in the city.

Amsterdam's demographics shifted dramatically in recent decades. Nearly a third of the city's residents are immigrants, hailing mainly from Turkey, North Africa, and Dutch colonies in the Caribbean. Strict social tolerance laws with harsh penalties were imposed to mollify the cultural tension that accompanied early immigration.

A Turn Toward the Past (2000-Present)

Recent years have seen some scaling back of Amsterdam's famed permissiveness. A third of the Red Light District's brothels were shut down in 2006 amid accusations of promoting criminality. In 2008, the central government ordered the city to shut down coffeehouses located within 500m of schools. The cultivation and sale of magic mushrooms was banned in the same year. In the past year, the government focused on banning tourists from its famous coffeeshops. For more information on this era-ending legislation, see the **Essentials** chapter.

CUSTOMS AND ETIQUETTE

We know you're expecting some culture shock in the Red Light District, but there's plenty to be aware of in your more "professional" encounters with Hollanders. When you are introduced to someone, a firm handshake is customary. Close friends greet each other with three kisses, *comme le style français.* When sharing a meal, men commonly wait for women to be seated.

Soft drugs and prostitution may be legal in Amsterdam, but abusers and law-breakers are punished harshly. Don't make a ruckus and get too carried away with your debauchery, and you'll be smooth-sailing. Please remember that public consumption of drugs remains illegal, as are all hard drugs, and that *Let's Go* does not recommend drug use.

HOLIDAYS AND FESTIVALS

HOLIDAY OR FESTIVAL	DESCRIPTION	DATE
Amsterdam International Fashion Week (AIFW)	A week of invitation-only catwalks and hoity-toity gatherings alongside public exhibitions and disco parties where you can show off your finest attire (and take the time to admire everyone else).	Late January
The Queen's Birthday	A day of national pride, with orange clothing and street parties everywhere. Though Queen Beatrix was actually born in January, she decided to keep the holiday on the springtime birthdate of the previous queen (her mother).	April 30 (April 29 if the 30th is a Sunday)
World Press Photo Exhibit	*Oude Kerk* hosts this celebration of the world's best photojournalism. Combines disturbing images of warfare with the serene beauty of the natural world.	Late April to mid-June
WWII Remembrance Day	A solemn day to remember the Netherlands' WWII victims. Two minutes of silence are observed at 8pm.	May 4
Liberation Day	A day of public festivities to celebrate the country's liberation from Nazi occupation.	May 5
National Windmill Day	Windmills throw open their doors, and many have special (often educational) events.	2nd Tuesday in May
Amsterdam Gay Pride	Three days of tolerance and partying, with a parade and street festivals for all sexual orientations.	Early August
Aalsmeer Flower Parade	Flower floats, flower art, and flower power in the world's tulip capital.	Early September
High Times Cannabis Cup	One long tokefest. At the end of the festival, awards are given to the best hash and marijuana.	November
Sinterklaas Eve	Dutch Santa Claus delivers candy and gifts to nice Dutch children. According to local lore, naughty kids are kidnapped (hope you're on the nice list).	December 5

FOOD AND DRINK

The typical Dutch *ontbijt* (breakfast) consists of bread topped with cold cuts and slices of local cheese, and a dab of *appelstroop* (syrup made from apple juice). If you're looking to satisfy your morning sweet tooth, top your toast with *hagelslag* (chocolate, anise, or fruit-flavored sprinkles). Of course, a strong cup of *kaffie* (coffee) is a favorite way to kick off the day.

Lunch (we'll let you figure out the translation of that yourself) includes rolls, sandwiches, or soup, eaten at one of the city's thousands of cafes. *Erwtensoep* (pea soup) is a cold-weather favorite and is often made with chunks of smoked sausage. You might also find *uitsmijter,* or Dutch fried eggs sunny-side-up (for some reason the name translates to "out-thrower" or "bouncer," as in the doorman at a club). A *broodje haring* (herring sandwich) garnished with onions and pickles is particularly tasty—you'll find one at fish stalls throughout the city.

Diner is served in Dutch homes around 5 or 6pm. A meat entree is traditionally accompanied by two vegetable side dishes, though you might encounter a *stamppot*, which combines meat, vegetables, and gravy in a mash. Amsterdam is also home to many Indonesian restaurants, a tasty relic of Dutch colonialism.

For dessert, you will find fruit, yogurt, or a cold custard followed by *kaffie*. The distinction between cafes and bars doesn't exist in the Netherlands. Cafes serve *kaffie* by day and beer by night. You can order a Heineken on its own turf, or sample some of the other famous Dutch pale lagers. A frosty *witbeer* (white beer) hits the spot after a long day of prowling the streets. *Eet smakelijk!* (Enjoy your meal!)

ART AND ARCHITECTURE

Amsterdam is world-renowned for its art, and with good reason. Dutch painters innovated the departure from the Gothic style of the Middle Ages, sparked the Northern Renaissance, perfected oil painting, and came up with the solution to global hunger (well maybe not yet, but give them time).

The First Dutch Masters

Jan van Eyck is sure to top any list of Amsterdam's best-known painters. In the 15th century, van Eyck was one of the first painters to use oil paint as a medium and impressed the art world with renderings of detailed architecture and realistic humans in long, multicolored robes. Keep your eyes peeled for reproductions of Amsterdam's most beloved knocked-up lady in green, featured in **The Arnolfini Portrait** (the original is in London's National Gallery). While van Eyck's paintings are prized by museums around the world, you'll find a select few on display at the **Rijksmuseum.**

Hieronymus Bosch, aside from bearing one of the hardest-to-spell names in all of art history, put his artistic whims to good work and left behind the Flemish style that van Eyck exemplified. His passion for originality carried him toward the cloud of surrealism some 400 years before the Surrealist movement really got off the ground. Though his paintings are notable for their departure from traditional technique, Bosch's mental stability might be called into question due to of the number of fantastical demons and hellish punishments he depicted with his brush. This guy was either uncomfortably preoccupied with hell or did some serious sinning in his spare time.

Golden Stars

During the Protestant Reformation of the 17th century, the Church stopped funding religious paintings, liberating artists from all that cumbersome Catholic symbolism. Dutch painters turned their gaze down from the heavens, up from hell, and right into the realm of the living. Many small paintings commissioned by bourgeois Flemish families depicted small, laughing children with kittens, their great-great uncles, and other semi-embarassing portraits. Looking at these paintings, it's easy to imagine a Dutch mother pulling one off the mantle when a potential suitor came to visit. "Remember when you were just a wee tyke and couldn't keep your hands off that pussy cat? You were such a little smidgeon-widgeon..." Mothers, it turns out, are remarkably similar across the ages.

The undisputed star of this Dutch Golden Age has to be **Rembrandt Harmenszoon van Rijn.** Though his style evolved over the course of his career, Rembrandt's paintings are marked by their masterful realism and the illusion of movement in his scenes. Initially celebrated by his compatriots, Rembrandt alienated his clientele when his art took an experimental turn. He was forced to declared bankruptcy and eventually died in poverty. Fortunately, his reputation has endured better than his finances, and you can get up close and personal with **The Night Watch** and **Landscape with a Stone Bridge 2** at the Rijksmuseum.

Johannes Vermeer, Rembrant's contemporary, is celebrated for creating windows into everday life of average 17th-century people. Among Vermeer's most renowned works is **Girl with a Pearl Earring,** widely hailed as the *Mona Lisa* of the north. If you're more into moving pictures than their still predecessors, consider Netflixing the 2003 film starring Scarlett Johansson, but this remarkable canvas is worth putting down the remote and getting your butt over to the Mauritshuis museum in The Hague.

Architecture: Bridge Over Troubled Water

Amsterdam itself is something of an architectural miracle. The city's often-aquatic geography forced architects to be creative. Canalside houses were built with many large windows to help keep the weight of the buildings from sinking them into the ground. Tight quarters forced the Dutch to build tall and skinny, giving rise to the city's winding and characteristically narrow streets. Homes were often built at frightening angles to allow large pieces of furniture to be hoisted through windows without hitting the buildings. The hooks that served as pulleys still stick out from just about every canal house, so watch your head as you wander narrow alleys. There's nothing like a piano landing on your head to ruin a perfectly good day of galumphing about the city.

SPORTS AND RECREATION

Feet and Balls

Soccer is, unsurprisingly, Amsterdam's biggest professional sport. The **Amsterdamsche Football Club Ajax** (AFC Ajax or Ajax for short), founded in 1900, is named after the legendary Greek hero, famed for his ability to toss boulders and leap between ships. This is a *voetbal* team anyone would be scared to mess with in the center circle, and for good reason: Ajax was ranked by the International Federation of Football History and Statistics as the seventh most successful European club of the 20th century. Don't be afraid to don your white shorts (anything but tightie-whities, please) and white jersey with single vertical red stripe to cheer on the two-time World Cup winners. Ajax plays in the Amsterdam ArenA (not a typo). While Ajax hasn't won an international title since 1995, that shouldn't stop you from screaming yourself hoarse at the ArenA, pint in hand.

Gender Unity?

Amsterdam is the birthplace of **Korfball,** a hybrid of basketball and soccer that makes strides to promote gender unity: each team must be composed of four men and four women. Players score points by tossing a soccer ball (made with more grip and bounce than the kind you kick) into the other team's *korf* (basket) attached to a 3m high pole. The court is divided in half with two men and two women of each team, playing side by side. Players may not switch zones, so all face-offs are man-on-man and woman-on-woman. When it burst on the scene in 1902, korfball generated quite a bit of controversy for mandating that men and women share the field. Players suffered accusations of immorality, especially because the female uniforms showed bare knees and ankles (the horror!). Korfball is now played in 57 countries (including the USA), but the Netherlands has won every Korfball World Championship title since the competition's inception in 1978, with the exception of 1991, when Belgium triumphed.

Beyond Tourism

If you are reading this, then you are a member of an elite group—and we don't mean "the literate." You're a student preparing for a semester abroad. You're taking a gap year to save the trees, the whales, or the dates. You're an 80-year-old woman who has devoted her life to egg-laying platypuses and what the hell is up with that. In short, you're a traveler, not a tourist; like any good spy, you don't just observe your surroundings—you become an active part of them.

Your mission, should you choose to accept it, is to study, volunteer, or work abroad as laid out in the dossier—er, chapter—below. We leave the rest (when to go, whom to bring, and how many *Arrested Development* DVDs to pack) in your hands. This message will self-destruct in five seconds. Good luck.

STUDYING

As you've hopefully figured out by now, Amsterdam has a lot more to offer than coffeehouses and peep-shows, including plenty of great educational opportunities.

Universities

Luckily for foreign students, most of Amsterdam's universities and academies teach courses in English. For those who want to learn Dutch, there are also plenty of language schools (see below) to help you talk your way through the city like a local.

International Programs

Council on International Educational Exchange (CIEE)
300 Fore St., Portland, ME 04101, USA
☎+1-800-407-8839; www.ciee.org

A three-week summer program gives students a chance to engage with social policy issues in the contemporary Netherlands, including multiculturalism, prostitution, drug policy, and abortion. CIEE also offers a term-time program hosted by the University of Amsterdam (UvA), with courses in gender studies, Dutch culture, and international relations.

▶ *i* Min. 3.0 GPA for term-time, 2.75 for summer. Junior status recommended. Ⓢ Summer $3150; semester $16,000; academic year $30,400. Scholarships available.

Institute for the International Education of Students (IES Abroad)
33 N. LaSalle St., 15th fl., Chicago, IL 60602, USA
☎+1-800-995-2300; www.iesabroad.org

IES Abroad offers a variety of programs. Undergrads can take English-language courses at the University of Amsterdam, in the arts, humanities, and social sciences (try "Cyberrelations and Cyberlove"). Graduates can enroll in a Pre-Law Certificate program in international law, again at the UvA. IES Abroad also offers a Research Experience program with lectures, field trips, and a final research paper. Finally, they can place students directly into local institutions—study jazz, performance, and music theory at the Conservatory of Amsterdam or hone your inner van Gogh at the Gerrit Rietveld Academie.

INTERNATIONAL STUDENT EXCHANGE PROGRAMS (ISEP)

1655 N. Fort Myer Dr., Ste. 400, Arlington, VA, 22209, USA

☎+1-703-504-9960; www.isep.org

If you're a student at one of their member universities, ISEP will help place you into one of its partner institutions abroad. Amsterdam has only two universities, and both are ISEP members. Both UvA and VU University Amsterdam offer courses in English on the arts, Christian studies, international business, and economics.

▶ *i* UvA programs require min. 3.0 GPA and min. 2yr. study of desired concentration. No on-campus housing. Ⓢ Summer $3350 (includes housing); semester $7850 (tuition only); academic year $13,050 (tuition only). VU University programs include monthly stipend for living and transportation.

Dutch Programs

University of Amsterdam (UvA)

Binnengasthuisstraat 9

☎020 525 33 33; www.english.uva.nl

Founded in 1632, UvA is the largest university in the Netherlands. Exchange students get a dedicated program with English courses in economics, business, science, law, and everything in between. Don't expect an authentic local academic experience: your classmate might be a clueless foreigner just like you. However, if you are already fluent in Dutch, you may enroll directly in regular courses. If your university lacks an exchange program, you can still pick up a Dutch education through UvA's certificate programs.

i Off-campus housing, varies by faculty. Shorter summer and winter programs are also offered. Ⓢ Exchange students pay tuition to their home university. Certificate programs €2000-4000.

VU University Amsterdam

De Boelelaan 1105

☎020 598 98 98; www.vu.nl

Though the "V" in the name stands for *vrije* (free), they mean freedom from church and state, not from tuition. Those whose schools have a partnership with VU University Amsterdam (see ISEP, above) get to study in a variety of English-taught faculties.

A new VU campus is currently under construction, but will not be completed until 2025. For now, enjoy studying in Zuidas, the business district in the south of the city.

▶ *i* A variety of housing available off campus. Ⓢ Students pay home tuition.

Hogeschool van Amsterdam, University of Applied Sciences (HVA)

Weesperzidje 190

☎020 525 67 77; www.international.hva.nl

Not technically a university, this *hogeschool* (university of applied science) offers a more technical and vocational education than its counterparts. If your school is one of its 250 international partners, you'll be able to take courses here, in fields like economics and management, nutrition, and education. Those with more time and dedication can stick around and earn their bachelor's at HvA.

▶ *i* HvA can offer a room if you apply early enough. Ⓢ Non-exchange programs €6800.

Language Schools

Even if everyone in Amsterdam seems to speak English already, there's no better way to dive into the city's culture than by picking up the local tongue. Here are a few of our favorites among the city's many language programs. Check out expat websites like **www.iamexpat.nl** and **www.iamsterdam.com** for even more listings.

ACT

Keizersgracht 620

☎020 423 58 69; www.act-taaltrainingen.nl/index-en.html

ACT has trained employees of big corporations like Nestle and Canon, but that shouldn't stop you from trying one of its six class levels. Those in a hurry can take the custom course path, which lets you cram six hours of study into a day, perfect for fluency in a flash.

▶ *i* Also offers culture courses. Ⓢ Contact info@act-taaltrainingen.nl for current course rates.

Talencoach

Keizersgracht 8

☎020 625 32 31; www.talencoach.nl

Run by a single teacher, Talencoach's programs all focus on

speed. Get ready to be "brain washed" into speaking (basic) Dutch in less than a week or take the Turbo Speed Course for two weeks of 3hr. sessions. Talencoach also offers free workshops and an e-book: *Why you hate Dutch and seven secrets to change it.*

▶ ⑤ Brain Wash Course €1495, Turbo Speed Course €1250.

Easy Dutch Plus
Leidsestraat 32
☎020 422 19 06; www.easydutchplus.com

Easy Dutch Plus offers lessons through 30hr. modules. Classes range from one-on-one to groups of up to eight, with decreasing hourly rates. If you're new in town and need a hand, Easy Dutch Plus can also help you find a room and offers a "personal integration guide" who will help you with translation and offer general advice.

▶ *i* Also offers translation services. 3-10 week courses. ⑤ Individual lessons €50 per hr.; 2-3 people €25 per hr.; 4-8 people €350 for 30hr., €650 for 60hr. Discounts if booking 2 modules.

Institute for Dutch as a Second Language (INNT at UvA)
Spuistraat 134
☎020 525 46 42; www.intt.uva.nl

Prospective UvA students should take note of this rigorous language institute. With six levels as well as winter and summer courses, you'll study in sync with the University academic calendar.

▶ ⑤ €4060, EU students €1672. Summer €320; winter course €1095. ⏰ Office open Tu-W 11:30am-12:30pm, Th 5:30-6:30pm, F 11:30am-12:30pm.

The School for Dutch
Weteringschans 84A
☎020 663 43 80; www.learndutch.com

With quips like "just do and don't think" and "talk first, grammar later," the School for Dutch makes its students as comfortable as possible so that they can unleash their conversational potential. Take the online test if you've already got a little Dutch under your belt, and once you enroll, join the online Learndutch Community to network with your expatriate classmates. Starting with the "Survival" course, you can work your way up to "Views and Opinions." You might find yourself discussing tulip economics in Dutch sooner than you think.

▶ $ €255-395 depending on level and schedule.

VOLUNTEERING

Save the Environment

Amsterdam's compassionate citizens anchor some of the world's most active environmental organizations. It may not be on-the-ground work, but you'll be living more comfortably than your friend saving echidnas in New Guinea.

Friends of the Earth International (FOEI)

Nieuwe Looiersstraat 31

☎020 550 73 00; www.foei.org

FOEI, "the world's largest grassroots environmental network" works to combat climate injustice and economic "neoliberal" exploitation, while promoting biodiversity and access to clean water. If you like your politics with a dash of leftist zeal, you'll feel right at home as a volunteer at FOEI's Amsterdam headquarters. Should the "small friendly office" feel too cramped, just remember that FOEI has branches in 76 other countries and over two million supporters worldwide.

▶ *i* Email media@foei.org to apply or inquire. Commitment 1-3 days per week.

World Wildlife Fund (WWF)

Driebergseweg 10, Zeist

☎0800 1962; www.wwf.org

If you're in Amsterdam for an extended time and looking to save the world on a flexible schedule, the WWF's branch offers three different levels of involvement. Join the Amsterdam Regioteam to lecture at local schools and help out with fundraising campaigns. Those who are footloose and want to go beyond Amsterdam can volunteer across the Netherlands as part of the Action Team. If you have a useful talent like translation or photography, sign up for the Talent Bank and the WWF will call you when it needs your help (it's like being a superhero!).

▶ *i* Must register in the online MijnWNF database.

Youth and the Community

Hart voor Amsterdam
Herengracht 218
☎020 637 53 75; www.hartvooramsterdam.nl

If you've gotten this far in the book, we assume you are fluent in English. Why not put that skill to work by teaching at-risk students? Through Hart voor Amsterdam's Native Speaker Project, you'll visit schools once a week to help young teens practice conversation and review for exams. The program even posts a regular lesson plan blog, so you don't even have to come up with your own curriculum. Just go forth and teach!

▶ *i* 2hrs. per week for 1-3 months. Email philippe@hartvooramsterdam.nl for more information.

Nowhere
Madurastraat 90
☎020 463 69 12; www.nowhere.nl

An artist's dream come true, Nowhere is a cultural youth center that trains budding painters, photographers, designers, and musicians and gives them the space to learn and flourish as artists. With master classes and workshops for volunteers, you can hone your skills with local talent while teaching the next generation of artists.

▶ *i* Knowledge of Dutch required.

Pink Point
Corner of Raadhuisstraat and Keizersgracht
☎020 428 10 70; www.pinkpoint.org

Pink Point began as an ice-cream cart converted to serve as an informational kiosk at the 1998 Gay Games. Now it welcomes tourists from its central location by the Anne Frank House, next to the busy Rosengracht, and provides information to help gay travelers get the most out of Amsterdam.

For the Undecided Altruist

Can't choose between teaching English, hosting concerts, or saving the environment? Want an even more original idea? These directories can help.

Vrijwilligers Central Amsterdam

Geldersekade 101

☎020 530 12 22; www.vca.nu

With five offices spread around the city, the Volunteers Center of Amsterdam welcomes Dutch-speakers and non-Dutch-speakers alike. The online database is in Dutch, but you can also schedule a walk-in consultation with English-speaking staff to learn about job opportunities, regulations, and workers' rights. With 3000 volunteers placed each year and over 1000 listings online, VCA is the best way to survey the Amsterdam volunteer scene.

▶ *i* Check website for walk-in consultation hours.

Markt.NL

Vondellaan 2, Utrecht

☎130 272 20 65; www.markt.nl

Primarily a job website for the whole of the Netherlands, www.markt.nl sometimes lists volunteer opportunities under their Sports and Leisure category.

WORKING

Long-Term Work

When funds run low and Amsterdam starts to look like a nice place to settle, you may want to find a long-term job. Temp agencies will help you pay the bills, and jobs in tourist info centers will keep you updated with the backpacking crowd, but think creatively for ways to experience Dutch culture outside of the tourist box. You'll find English jobs at some international companies, but knowledge of Dutch opens many more doors.

Teaching

Amsterdam is not the best place to find a job teaching English, since almost everybody here is already fluent. You'll find most opportunities in private, international schools, where prerequisites for teachers usually include a bachelor's degree, native speaking ability, and previous experience.

International School of Amsterdam

Sportlaan 45, Amstelveen

☎020 347 11 11; www.isa.nl

You'll find the children of Amsterdam's international elite at this pre-K-12 school, with over 50 countries represented on its suburban campus. The school usually has several job openings, some with immediate starting dates, but they prefer at least three years of previous teaching experience.

Katakura/WBLC

Havikshorst 30

☎020 612 27 27; www.katakura-wblc.nl

Founded in Japan, this language school offers Dutch language classes at its two Amsterdam locations, but you might be equally interested in its search for experienced native-English teachers.

KERN

Nieuwezijds Voorburgwal 44-I

☎020 520 07 40; www.e-kern.com

A multilingual translation, interpretation, and multimedia company with several branches across the world, KERN is looking for language teachers, translators, interpreters, and even interns. Use the online application to skip mailing the paper version to its Frankfurt headquarters.

Au Pair Work

Prospective au pairs must usually be 18-30, unmarried, and prepared with the required paperwork. Check that your au pair agency is recognized by the **Immigration and Naturalization Service** (http://english.ind.nl). **The Netherlands Au Pair Organization** provides local listings of member au pair agencies as well as a 24hr. emergency phoneline.

Great Au Pair

1329 Hwy. 395, Ste 10-333, Gardnerville, NV 89410, USA

☎+1-800-935-6303; www.greataupair.com

Great Au Pair lets you filter job listings by pay, duration, and accommodations, but keep in mind that postings are made by the host families themselves. Also provides a resourceful guide to being an au pair.

▶ *i* Must register to apply and contact host families.

House o Orange

Jan Van Nassaustraat 88, The Hague
☎070 324 59 03; www.house-o-orange.nl

A play on the name of the Dutch royal dynasty, this au pair agency has branches around the world but keeps it personal with its small staff and colorful website.

▶ *i* Fill out the online form to begin the 2-3 month application process, or email for more information. You'll receive a login for their website that lets you view their job listings.

InterExchange

161 6th Ave., New York, NY 10013, USA
☎+1-212-924-0446; www.interexchange.org

Make your time in Amsterdam more than just chasing after children and cleaning their rooms. InterExchange's program grants you funding for Dutch language classes, guarantees at least two days off each week, and confers membership in the "Au Pair Club" with meetings and field trips included.

▶ *i* 10-12 months. ⑤ Program fee $495.

Other Long-Term Work

Recruitment agencies *(uitzendbureaus)* are paid by employers, so you get to look for and apply to jobs for free. Watch out for the same agencies across different recruiters: you don't want to apply for the same job twice. Some also list internships.

Blue Lynx

Teleportboulevard 110
☎020 406 91 80; www.bluelynx.com

Besides offering the usual categories of location and job type, Blue Lynx lets you search for work by the languages that you speak. If you can speak Danish, Norwegian, Turkish, French, or German, in addition to English, you may be surprised by how many jobs in Amsterdam need trilingual skills.

▶ *i* Register online to upload a resume and create a profile.

Kelly Services

Overtoom 1
☎020 607 77 20; www.kelly.nl

An American company with branches across the world, including six in the Netherlands, Kelly Services links internationals with international companies and proudly claims that "Dutch

is not required," though its many listings without translations beg to differ.
- ▶ *i* Open to browsing, but create an online profile to apply.

Together Abroad
Beemsterhof 15, The Hague
☎062 296 67 37; www.togetherabroad.nl

Together Abroad's English-only website is a user-friendly starting point for any expatriate looking for a job in the Netherlands. Browse the listings (updated daily) and sign up for job-search and career-development workshops.
- ▶ *i* Group workshops €25; individual €40.

Undutchables
Westeinde 20
☎020 623 13 00; www.undutchables.nl

Catering to foreigners, this recruitment agency lets English-speaking job-seekers interview at one of their seven offices across the Netherlands, two of which are in Amsterdam.
- ▶ *i* Register online with your resume.

Short-Term Work

Want to make money but don't like long commitments? Check out the local and online recruitment agencies (above). If you're studying at a local school, you can also ask around the employment office of your university. Seasonal jobs pop up in cafes, bars, and restaurants, especially when the real tourists come in.

JoHo
Taksteeg 8
☎088 321 45 67; www.joho.nl/english

This Dutch youth-travel company calls itself "the starting point for internationals' dreams and deeds." Although its website can be a nightmare to navigate, JoHo's recruitment desk at its Amsterdam office can help connect you with potential employers. JoHo also provides travel insurance, banking services, a fair trade and travel store, and a Dutch and English book store (with job openings for volunteers), as well as links to other volunteer and work-abroad centers around the world.
- ▶ 🕐 Open 11:30am-5:30pm.

Boom Chicago

Leidseplein 12

☎020 530 02 32; www.boomchicago.nl

An American-style comedy club in the historic Leidseplein Theater, Boom Chicago presents (almost) nightly shows, with dinner and drink service. Openings are usually for box office (Dutch and English required) and promotion staff (bike required). If you think you're witty enough to make it to the stage, don't go to Amsterdam yet: Boom Chicago holds yearly auditions in Chicago and Los Angeles.

▶ *i* Contact jon@boomchicago.nl for audition information. See website for other openings.

Index

A
accommodations: 29–48; *see also* Accommodations Index
ACT: 162
Alto: 118
Amnesia: 122
Amsterdam 101: 151–158
Amsterdam Historical Museum: 55
Amsterdam Sex Museum: 54
Amsterdams Centrum voor Fotografie: 50
Anne Frank House: 57
architecture: 156
art: 156
arts and culture: 115–124
Azarius: 123

BC
Begijnhof: 56
beyond tourism: 159–170
Bijbels Museum: 61
Blue Lynx: 168
Boom Chicago: 119, 170
Brouwerij de Prael: 53
Brouwerij 't IJ: 71
Bush Doctor, The: 124
Canal Ring West: 12, 24
Cannabis College: 53
Central Canal Ring: 12, 23
classical music: 116
climate: 147
coffeeshops: 122
comedy theater: 119
comedy: 119
Concertgebouw: 116
Cotton Club: 118
Council on International Educational Exchange (CIEE): 160
customs: 154

DEF
Dam Square: 56
De Nieuwe Anita: 117
De Pijp: 15, 26
De Tweede Kamer: 123
Easy Dutch Plus: 163
Electric Ladyland: 63
essentials: 132–150
etiquette: 154
EYE Institute: 120
festivals: 155
film: 120
FOAM: 61
food: 73–93, 155; *see also* Restaurants Index
Friends of the Earth International (FOEI): 164

GH
Golden Bend: 62
Great Au Pair: 167
Hart voor Amsterdam: 165
health: 143
Heineken Experience: 68
history: 152
Hofjes: 64
Hogeschool van Amsterdam, University of Applied Sciences (HVA): 162
holidays: 155
Homomonument: 58
Hortus Botanicus: 72
hotels: *see* accommodations
House o Orange: 168

IJK
Institute for Dutch as a Second Language (INNT at UvA): 163

Institute for the International Education of Students (IES Abroad): 160
InterExchange: 168
International School of Amsterdam: 167
International Student Exchange Programs (ISEP): 161
itineraries: 16–17
Jodenbuurt: 15, 27
JoHo: 169
Joods Historisch Museum (Jewish Historical Museum): 70
Jordaan: 14, 24
Katakura/WBLC: 167
Kelly Services: 168
KERN: 167

LM

language: 148
Leidseplein: 13, 23
live music: 117
Maloe Melo: 118
Markt.NL: 166
measurements: 148
Melkweg: 117
money: 141
Multatuli Museum: 59
Museum Het Schip: 64
Museum Willet-Holthuysen: 62
Museumplein: 15, 25
Muziekgebouw aan't IJ: 116
Muziektheater: 116

NO

Nederlands Instituut voor Mediakunst: 60
neighborhoods: 10–16
Nieuwe Kerk: 54
Nieuwe Zijd: 11, 22
Nieuwmarkt: 50
nightlife: 94–114; see also Nightlife Index
Nowhere: 165
Ons' Lieve Heer op Solder: 52
Oost-Indisch Huis: 51
opera: 116
Oude Kerk: 51
Oude Zijd: 10, 22
Oud-West: 14, 28

PQR

Paradiso: 118
Paradox: 122
Pathe Tuschinski: 121
Pink Point: 165
planning tips: 9, 133
Plantage: 15, 27
recreation: 158
Red Light District: 11, 22
Rembrandt House Museum: 71
Rembrandtplein: 13, 23
restaurants: see food
Rijksmuseum: 66

S

safety: 143
Sarphatipark: 68
Sauna Deco: 121
saunas: 121
Scheepvaartbuurt: 12, 24
School for Dutch, The : 163
shopping: 125–131; see also Shopping Index
sights: 49–72
spas: 121
sports: 158
Stadsschouwburg: 119
Stedelijk Museum Bureau Amsterdam (SMBA): 63
studying: 160

TUV

Talencoach: 162
theater: 119
Thermos: 121

together abroad: 169
transportation: 138, 139
Tropenmuseum: 70
Tweedy: 124
Undutchables: 169
University of Amsterdam (UvA): 161
Van Gogh Museum: 65
Verzetsmuseum (Dutch Resistance Museum): 69
volunteering: 164
Vondelpark: 15, 25, 67

Vrijwilligers Central Amsterdam: 166
VU University Amsterdam: 161

WXYZ

Westergasfabriek Park: 65
Westerkerk: 58
Westerpark: 14, 28
when to go: 10
working: 166
World Wildlife Fund (WWF): 164

Accommodations Index

Aivengo Youth Hostel: 34
Backstage Hotel: 40
Bicycle Hotel: 47
Bob's Youth Hostel: 34
Bridge Hotel: 48
City Hotel: 42
Durty Nelly's Hostel: 31
Flying Pig Downtown: 33
Flying Pig Uptown: 46
Frederic Rent-a-Bike: 36
Freeland: 41
Golden Bear, The: 39
Greenhouse Effect Hotel, The: 31
Hemp Hotel: 39
Hermitage Hotel: 48
Hostel Aroza: 35
Hotel Abba: 45
Hotel Acacia: 44
Hotel Asterisk: 40
Hotel Belga: 38
Hotel Bema: 46
Hotel Brouwer: 35
Hotel Clemens: 37
Hotel Groenendael: 35
Hotel Hegra: 38
Hotel Internationaal: 32

Hotel Jupiter: 45
Hotel Kap: 39
Hotel Monopole: 43
Hotel Museumzicht: 47
Hotel My Home: 36
Hotel Pax: 38
Hotel Quentin: 42
Hotel the Veteran: 42
Hotel Van Onna: 44
Hotel Vijaya: 33
Hotel Vivaldi: 47
Hotel Westertoren: 37
Hotel Winston: 32
International Budget Hostel: 41
King Hotel: 41
Meeting Point Youth Hostel: 32
Nadia Hotel: 37
Old Nickel Hotel: 33
Ramenas Hotel: 36
Shelter City: 30
Shelter Jordaan: 43
Stayokay Amsterdam Stadsdoelen (HI): 30
Stayokay Amsterdam Vondelpark: 45

Restaurants Index

B and B Lunchroom: 82
Bazar: 91
Bella Storia: 87
Bird: 75
Bojo: 83
Burgermeester: 92
Cafe De Pijp: 90
Cafe Nassau: 89
Cafe Schuim: 76
Cafe Vertigo: 89
De Avondmarkt: 88
De Bakkerswinkel: 75
De Kaaskamer: 80
De Soepwinkel: 91
De Vliegende Schotel: 86
De Zotte: 83
Eetkunst Asmara: 92
Golden Temple: 82
Harlem: Drinks and Soul Food: 78
Het Ijspaleis: 90
In de Waag: 75
J. J. Ooijevaar: 84
La Place: 77
Latei: 74
Le Sud: 79
Open Cafe-Restaurant: 78
Pancake Bakery, The: 81
Pantry, The: 83
Pasta Tricolore: 90
Peperwortel: 88
Plancius: 93
Rainarai: 85
Ristorante Caprese: 77
Ristorante Pizzeria Firenze: 85
Rose's Cantina: 85
Si Chaun Kitchen: 76
Sie Joe: 77
'Skek: 74
Soep en Zo: 93
'T Kuyltje: 79
Tasca Bellota: 79
Tomatillo: 87
Toscanini: 86
Van Dobben: 84
Vennington: 81
Warung Spang Makandra: 91
Wild Moa Pies: 92
Winkel: 86
Zuivere Koffie: 81

Nightlife Index

Belgique: 100
Bitterzoet: 100
Blauwe Theehuis: 113
Bourbon Street 106
Cafe "Oost-West": 96
Cafe Aen't Water: 98
Cafe Brandon: 103
Cafe Brecht: 103
Cafe Chris: 111
Cafe de Engelbewaarder: 95
Cafe de Jaren: 96
Chocolate Bar: 113
Club NL: 101
Club Winston: 98
Dansen bij Jansen: 100
De Duivel: 108
De Pieper 106
De Prins: 102
de Sluyswacht: 114
Dulac: 102
Durty Nelly's Pub 97
Escape: 108
Festina Lente: 110
Getto: 98
Gollem: 100
Het Elfde Gebod: 95
Kingfisher: 114
Lellebel: 109

Mankind: 104
Melkweg 106
Montmartre: 109
OT301: 111
Pacific Parc 112
Paradiso105
Prik: 99
Punto Latino: 107
Saarein: 110

Studio 80: 107
Sugar Factory: 105
't Smalle 110
Tara PUB, The : 101
Thirsty Dogg: 102
Trouw Amsterdam: 113
Vive la Vie: 108
Weber: 105
Wynand Fockink: 97

Shopping Index

Albert Cuypmarkt: 128
American Book Center: 127
Concerto: 130
Dappermarkt: 129
Lady Day: 128
Laura Dols: 128
Noordermarkt: 129
Petticoat: 128

South Miami Plaza: 130
SPRMRKT: 126
Studio 88: 126
The Book Exchange: 127
The English Bookshop: 127
The Old Man: 131
Velvet Music: 131
Vezjun: 126

AMSTERDAM ACKNOWLEDGMENTS

SPENCER THANKS: To Linda for fomenting revolution. To Kat, Nicole, Beebs, and RoRo for risking life and limb to bring us intrepid reporting, sterling research, and rib-cracking marginalia. To the legendary sass of Billy and Michael. To Chris for keeping us on shedule. To Iya for being the second most famous Georgian I know. To trivia for simultaneously improving and decimating my self-esteem. To the Red-Headed League. To Proletariat Coffee (and capitalist coffee too). To Electric Ladyland. To Kentucky's finest bourbon, to Cambridge summers and porch-sitting, to Jack Spicer. To CuddlePod, Animal Farm, Whitney's tattoo artistry, Joe's futon, venn diagrams, the office snuggie, headgear of oracular origins, and sleep. To my parents. And most of all to Tanjore Tuesdays for fueling LGHQ through a long, hot summer.

LINDA THANKS: The cause for meaning. The Frevolution and those classy Tuesday nights. Israel, for being Israel. Amy for sanity. Michael, the master of the winky face, for tension and adorableness. Mp styles for sweet jamz and leading the charge. Billy for conducting the chorus of wahh. Spencer for the glory and the primates and the cuddles. Kat for bearing wonderful gifts and being the best RW ever. TWiz Khalifa because he deserves a thumbpick somewhere. That man at Dunks for not making me explain myself. All Comrades, all around the world, we salute you. JTR.

ABOUT LET'S GO

The Student Travel Guide

Let's Go publishes the world's favorite student travel guides, written entirely by Harvard students. Armed with pens, notebooks, and a few changes of clothes stuffed into their backpacks, our student researchers go across continents, through time zones, and above expectations to seek out invaluable travel experiences for our readers. Because we are a completely student-run company, we have a unique perspective on how students travel, where they want to go, and what they're looking to do when they get there. If your dream is to grab a machete and forge through the jungles of Costa Rica, we can take you there. If you'd rather bask in the Riviera sun at a beachside cafe, we'll set you a table. In short, we write for readers who know that there's more to travel than tour buses. To keep up, visit our website, www.letsgo.com, where you can sign up to blog, post photos from your trips, and connect with the Let's Go community.

Traveling Beyond Tourism

We're on a mission to provide our readers with sharp, fresh coverage packed with socially responsible opportunities to go beyond tourism. Each guide's Beyond Tourism chapter shares ideas about responsible travel, study abroad, and how to give back to the places you visit while on the road. To help you gain a deeper connection with the places you travel, our fearless researchers scour the globe to give you the heads-up on both world-renowned and off-the-beaten-track opportunities. We've also opened our pages to respected writers and scholars to hear their takes on the countries and regions we cover, and asked travelers who have worked, studied, or volunteered abroad to contribute first-person accounts of their experiences.

Fifty-Two Years of Wisdom

Let's Go has been on the road for 52 years and counting. We've grown a lot since publishing our first 20-page pamphlet to Europe in 1960, but five decades and 60 titles later, our witty, candid guides are still researched and written entirely by students on shoestring budgets who know that train strikes, stolen luggage, food poisoning, and marriage proposals are all part of a day's work. Meanwhile, we're still bringing readers fresh new features, such as a student-life section with advice on how and where to meet students from around the world; a revamped, user-friendly layout for our listings; and greater emphasis on the experiences that make travel abroad a rite of passage for readers of all ages. And, of course, this year's 16 titles—including five brand-new guides—are still brimming with editorial honesty, a commitment to students, and our irreverent style.

The Let's Go Community

More than just a travel guide company, Let's Go is a community that reaches from our headquarters in Cambridge, MA, all across the globe. Our small staff of dedicated student editors, writers, and tech nerds comes together because of our shared passion for travel and our desire to help other travelers get the most out of their experience. We love it when our readers become part of the Let's Go community as well—when you travel, drop us a postcard (67 Mt. Auburn St., Cambridge, MA 02138, USA), send us an email (feedback@letsgo.com), or sign up on our website (www.letsgo.com) to tell us about your adventures and discoveries.

For more information, updated travel coverage, and news from our researcher team, visit us online at www.letsgo.com.

LET'S GO BUDGET

TAKE A LET'S GO BUDGET GUIDE TO EUROPE

LET'S GO BUDGET AMSTERDAM
978-1-61237-015-6

LET'S GO BUDGET ATHENS
978-1-61237-005-7

LET'S GO BUDGET BARCELONA
978-1-61237-014-9

LET'S GO BUDGET BERLIN
978-1-61237-006-4

LET'S GO BUDGET FLORENCE
978-1-61237-007-1

LET'S GO BUDGET ISTANBUL
978-1-61237-008-8

LET'S GO BUDGET LONDON
978-1-61237-013-2

LET'S GO BUDGET MADRID
978-1-61237-009-5

LET'S GO BUDGET PARIS
978-1-61237-011-8

LET'S GO BUDGET PRAGUE
978-1-61237-010-1

LET'S GO BUDGET ROME
978-1-61237-012-5

ALL LET'S GO BUDGET GUIDEBOOKS ARE $9.99.
Let's Go also publishes guides to individual countries that are available at bookstores and online retailers.

For more information: **visit LETSGO.COM**
JOIN THE DISCUSSION WITH LET'S GO ON **FACEBOOK** AND **TWITTER**

HELPING LET'S GO. If you want to share your discoveries, suggestions, or corrections, please drop us a line. We appreciate every piece of correspondence, whether a postcard, a 10-page email, or a coconut. Visit Let's Go at www.letsgo.com or send an email to:

feedback@letsgo.com, subject: "Let's Go Budget Amsterdam"

Address mail to:

Let's Go Budget Amsterdam, 67 Mount Auburn St., Cambridge, MA 02138, USA

In addition to the invaluable travel advice our readers share with us, many are kind enough to offer their services as researchers or editors. Unfortunately, our charter enables us to employ only currently enrolled Harvard students.
Maps © Let's Go and Avalon Travel
Design Support by Jane Musser, Sarah Juckniess, Tim McGrath
Production and Interior design by Darren Alessi
Photos © Let's Go, Katharine Vidt and Beatrice Franklin, photographers

Distributed by Publishers Group West.
Printed in Canada by Friesens Corp.

Let's Go Budget Amsterdam Copyright © 2012 by Let's Go, Inc. All rights reserved. No part of this book may be used or reproduced in any manner whatsoever without written permission except in the case of brief quotations embodied in critical articles or reviews. Let's Go is available for purchase in bulk by institutions and authorized resellers.

ISBN-13: 978-1-61237-015-6
ISBN-10: 1-61237-015-2
First edition
10 9 8 7 6 5 4 3 2 1

Let's Go Budget Amsterdam is written by Let's Go Publications, 67 Mt. Auburn St., Cambridge, MA 02138, USA.

Let's Go® and the LG logo are trademarks of Let's Go, Inc.

LEGAL DISCLAIMER. For 50 years, Let's Go has published the world's favorite budget travel guides, written entirely by students and updated periodically based on the personal anecdotes and travel experiences of our student writers. Although every effort was made to ensure that the information was correct at the time of going to press, the author and publisher do not assume and hereby disclaim any liability to any party for any loss or damage caused by errors, omissions, or any potential travel disruption due to labor or financial difficulty, whether such errors or omissions result from negligence, accident, or any other cause.

ADVERTISING DISCLAIMER. All advertisements appearing in Let's Go publications are sold by an independent agency not affiliated with the editorial production of the guides. Advertisers are never given preferential treatment, and the guides are researched, written, and published independent of advertising. Advertisements do not imply endorsement of products or services by Let's Go, and Let's Go does not vouch for the accuracy of information provided in advertisements.

If you are interested in purchasing advertising space in a Let's Go publication, contact Edman & Company at 1-203-656-1000.

QUICK REFERENCE

YOUR GUIDE TO LET'S GO ICONS

🞕	Let's Go recommends	☎	Phone numbers	≠	Directions
i	Other hard info	Ⓢ	Prices	🕗	Hours

IMPORTANT PHONE NUMBERS

EMERGENCY: ☎112			
Amsterdam	☎911	London	☎999
Barcelona	☎092	Madrid	☎092
Berlin	☎110	Paris	☎17
Florence	☎113	Prague	☎158
Istanbul	☎155	Rome	☎113

TEMPERATURE CONVERSIONS

°CELSIUS	-5	0	5	10	15	20	25	30	35	40
°FAHRENHEIT	23	32	41	50	59	68	77	86	95	104

MEASUREMENT CONVERSIONS

1 inch (in.) = 25.4mm	1 millimeter (mm) = 0.039 in.
1 foot (ft.) = 0.305m	1 meter (m) = 3.28 ft.
1 mile (mi.) = 1.609km	1 kilometer (km) = 0.621 mi.
1 pound (lb.) = 0.454kg	1 kilogram (kg) = 2.205 lb.
1 gallon (gal.) = 3.785L	1 liter (L) = 0.264 gal.